Don's passion for prison ministry drove him to really engage with the outcast—the least, lost, last, and lonely. He loves blessing them corporately with good news while fellowshipping with them individually, especially on death row. Over time, these inmates became friends. This book is a snapshot into some of the lives of those he met and befriended, allowing the reader to see redemption and deliverance through Don's love and devotion "just for Jesus."

—Bill Morgan
CEO and Consulting Principal, Avistas

I introduced Don to Puerto Rican chaplains and translated for him in all the Spanish-speaking services, and we saw many, many accept Christ over the years. You will love the stories in this book.

—Virginia Martinez
Former Probation Officer

I was blessed and honored to meet Don Dickerman and host him in our many Puerto Rican jails and prisons. Along with fellow brother and chaplain Ariel Otero, we traveled our beautiful island to preach and fellowship.

—Angel "Pocho" Hernandez
Director of Chaplains

DEATH ROW
REDEMPTION

Untold Stories
of Forgiven Felons

DEATH ROW REDEMPTION

DON DICKERMAN

CHARISMA HOUSE

DEATH ROW REDEMPTION by Don Dickerman
Published by Charisma House, an imprint of Charisma Media
1150 Greenwood Blvd., Lake Mary, Florida 32746

Copyright © 2025 by Don Dickerman. All rights reserved.

Unless otherwise noted, all Scripture quotations are taken from the New King James Version®. Copyright © 1982 by Thomas Nelson. Used by permission. All rights reserved.

Scripture quotations marked ESV are from The ESV® Bible (The Holy Bible, English Standard Version®), copyright © 2001 by Crossway, a publishing ministry of Good News Publishers. Used by permission. All rights reserved.

Scripture quotations marked KJV are from the King James Version of the Bible.

Scripture quotations marked NASB are taken from the (NASB®) New American Standard Bible®, Copyright © 1960, 1971, 1977, 1995 by The Lockman Foundation. Used by permission. All rights reserved. www.lockman.org

Scripture quotations marked NIV are taken from the Holy Bible, New International Version®, NIV®. Copyright © 1973, 1978, 1984, 2011 by Biblica, Inc.® Used by permission of Zondervan. All rights reserved worldwide. www.zondervan.com. The "NIV" and "New International Version" are trademarks registered in the United States Patent and Trademark Office by Biblica, Inc.®

While the author has made every effort to provide accurate, up-to-date source information at the time of publication, statistics and other data are constantly updated. Neither the publisher nor the author assumes any responsibility for errors or for changes that occur after publication. Further, the publisher and author do not have any control over and do not assume any responsibility for third-party websites or their content.

For more resources like this, visit MyCharismaShop.com and the author's website at liberatedliving.info.

Cataloging-in-Publication Data is on file with the Library of Congress.

International Standard Book Number: 978-1-63641-518-5
E-book ISBN: 978-1-63641-519-2

1 2025
Printed in the United States of America

Most Charisma Media products are available at special quantity discounts for bulk purchase for sales promotions, premiums, fund-raising, and educational needs. For details, call us at (407) 333-0600 or visit our website at charismamedia.com.

The author has made every effort to provide accurate accounts of events, but he acknowledges that others may have different recollections of these events.

Images courtesy of Don Dickerman. Used with permission.

CONTENTS

Foreword by David Berkowitz xi

Introduction: God Tricked Me. xiii

Chapter 1   Execution—James David Raulerson 1

Chapter 2   Almost Executed: Thomas Gerald Laney 19

Chapter 3   Texas-Sized Forgiveness: Arnold Munoz 43

Chapter 4   "The Meanest Guy in Prison": Jim Cavanagh . . . 55

Chapter 5   Real Demon Possession: David Berkowitz 61

Chapter 6   The Widow: Betty Lou Beets 73

Chapter 7   Women on Death Row: Frances Newton, Pam
Perillo, and Karla Faye Tucker. 77

Chapter 8   The Meanest Man in South Carolina:
Donald "Pee Wee" Gaskins 95

Chapter 9   Serial Killer: Ted Bundy 99

Chapter 10   Vengeful Irishman: Eddie Ferncombe 105

Chapter 11   Twenty-Five to Life: Laurie Kellogg 117

Chapter 12   Masterminded the Murder of Her Parents:
Sheryl Sohn. 123

Chapter 13   The Man Who Shot John Lennon:
Mark David Chapman 143

Chapter 14   The Hillside Strangler: Kenneth Bianchi 151

Chapter 15   The Monster: Willie Bosket Jr. 155

Chapter 16   Cult Leader: Charles Manson 165

Chapter 17   Drug Cartel Hit Man: Jesse Ramirez 175

Chapter 18   Execution—Jimmy Lee Gray 181

Chapter 19   Execution—Foreign Jurisdiction 199

A Note from the Author 217

Notes 218

About the Author 222

FOREWORD

WHEN I WAS finally arrested on a sweltering night in August 1977, a squad of detectives pointing their guns at my head from every direction, it was a miracle that the Lord Jesus kept those cops from shooting me on the spot. Don, it seemed the Lord would not allow them to pull the triggers.

I got involved in satanism after serving in the army. At twenty-one, I was looking to start a new life and make new friends, as my old companions had moved on in the three years I was gone. Unfortunately, the friends I made were not good ones. From there, I drifted down a path that led to six murders and the wounding of seven others in what was a demonically driven killing spree.

My story has been chronicled by newspapers and other media outlets since the crimes took place in the mid-seventies. However, to this date, the public has yet to understand the demonic aspects of my case. I came to a place in my deceived heart where I began to worship a high-ranking demon known as Samhain, the god of the druids. Samhain demanded human sacrifices to appease him. That's how delusional I had become.

In these pages you'll read about how Jesus saved me, as well as many others, in a place some people would consider "too far gone," the place of last resort—prison. But no one is beyond the reach of Jesus.

With love in Christ,

—DAVID BERKOWITZ
WALLKILL CORRECTIONAL FACILITY
WALLKILL, NY

Introduction

GOD TRICKED ME

I KNEW FORTY YEARS ago I would be writing this book. I was meeting so many notorious inmates, and it was not because I was seeking them. It seemed as though God was putting me in contact with the meanest of all inmates. I knew then as I know now that no one—not you, not me, not a drug dealer, not a serial killer on death row—is too far gone for Jesus to reach them and set them free.

I felt a definite call to go into the prison to evangelize—of that I was sure. I had been sure of my call since my first day in a prison. Many times, when people ask me, "Why prisons?" I say, "God tricked me." I was valedictorian of my graduating class, and I was ready to be the next Billy Graham. Just rent me a stadium and turn me loose. No one could have told me that I would be casting out demons and preaching in prisons. Those two ministries would probably have been my last choice.

But I would not change anything.

I had been asked to serve as interim pastor of Shady Oaks

xiii

Baptist Church in Hurst, Texas. God blessed the church during my time there, and we led in baptisms for Tarrant County (a statistic I didn't even know was kept).

Then one night I got a phone call from a lady in the church: "My husband just shot a man!" That led me to go with this young wife to visit her husband in one of Texas's many prisons, the Ferguson facility in Midway, Texas. I already thought I knew what the inmates were like—hard-faced and scarred with cold, uncaring eyes. Instead, I saw guys who looked like me and my two boys. I saw parents visiting their children. What a surprise!

The man we went to see asked me to come preach in their chapel. I didn't even know they had chapels and church services in prison. The inmate, Kenny, called for his chaplain—Rev. Dick Kastner, still a good friend—to come meet me. I eventually went there to preach, and that led me to preach in more than 850 different prisons in the Caribbean, Europe, and all over the United States and Canada, some as many as a hundred times.

Why wouldn't I change it? Because I see miracles. I see things at the hand of God that I *never* saw in the local churches. I see the truth that no one is so far gone they can't be redeemed by the Savior.

Meeting these notorious inmates and seeing their lives changed by the power of God began to be almost commonplace, and I knew then that I would be writing this book. When I shared their stories with friends, I always got the same response: "You need to write a book." I prayed much about this, and I believe I heard seven words clearly from the Lord: "Write the book; I will bless it."

I hope that by reading *Death Row Redemption* you too will

God Tricked Me

see the truth that no one is so far gone they can't be redeemed by the Savior.

> For God so loved the world that He gave His only begotten Son, that whoever believes in Him should not perish but have everlasting life. For God did not send His Son into the world to condemn the world, but that the world through Him might be saved. He who believes in Him is not condemned.
>
> —JOHN 3:16–18

Chapter 1

EXECUTION—
JAMES DAVID RAULERSON

O N APRIL 27, 1975, J. D. Raulerson and his cousin, Jerry Tant, forced their way inside the Sailmaker restaurant on Atlantic Boulevard in Jacksonville, Florida. It was a little after 11:00 p.m., closing time, when the restaurant manager unlocked the back door to let an employee out to empty trash cans. Inside, a waitress was cleaning cocktail tables, and another employee was counting the day's receipts—a routine that took place each night.

Outside the back door, the restaurant employee got a gun stuck in his face, and two armed men slammed the door open and bolted into the restaurant. Within thirty minutes, two people were wounded, and two were killed.

Raulerson, though never convicted of or charged with the offense, allegedly forced a waitress to disrobe and sexually assaulted her as Tant held the other employees at gunpoint.

Two Jacksonville police officers happened to be in the area when the robbery was taking place and surprised the two would-be robbers. A gun battle ensued. Officer Michael Stewart was hit by a bullet and killed. Also killed was Jerry Tant, Raulerson's cousin.

Officer James English was hit in the chest area with a bullet, but he was the recipient of a miracle instead of death. The bullet intended for his heart struck a metal pen in his pocket and was deflected aside.

When charges were filed, Raulerson was indicted for capital murder, a charge that could mean death in Florida's electric chair. At the trial, prosecutors maintained that Raulerson made a living out of robbing and produced evidence in that police found more than $10,000—money that belonged to a Tallahassee restaurant—in Raulerson's Corvette at a beach motel. Raulerson was convicted of capital murder.

ALMOST TEN YEARS ON DEATH ROW

Raulerson maintained that he never shot anyone. He claimed to the bitter end that Officer English shot Stewart by mistake. He once asked me, "Don, if they are so certain about this, why not do the ballistics test? Think about it—they could do the test and shut me up. They know I didn't do it. I didn't do it. I don't kill. I don't kill animals."

He tried in vain to somehow get the investigation reopened. He wrote letters to the news networks and investigative reporters. He asked for them to get ballistics experts to check the bullet that killed Stewart. (Ballistics test results were used to convict him; Raulerson challenged those tests.) It didn't seem to matter to those who viewed the case from a distance whether he pulled the trigger. He was guilty of robbery, and he was responsible for the unfortunate murder that resulted.

There were bitter feelings between police personnel and Raulerson right up to the day of the execution. In 1979, after the execution of John Spenkelink, Jacksonville police officers were criticized for selling T-shirts with a picture of the electric chair and the words "Raulerson, you're next..."[1] They sold T-shirts again as the execution became a reality.

Raulerson spent almost ten years on death row. Death row time is not easy for anyone—not for the family and loved ones of the victim of the crime, not for the family and loved ones of the convicted, and certainly not for the convicted. Just mention the death penalty, and you have controversy. In America today there is an overwhelming belief in capital punishment. I believe anger over crime in general is partially responsible for this feeling. We are all upset over rising crime and a justice system that appears to favor the criminal.

People who oppose the death penalty are often classified

as left-wing liberals. Some even think they condone crime because of their stand. I have never met anyone who believed that. It is a useless argument. No one wins; no one changes their thinking.

I can't speak with much experience about protesters; I am not one. I was there, inside the witness box, when this man was executed. I got to know J. D. Raulerson through the mail. I receive a large volume of mail because of our nationwide ministry to prisons and monthly newsletter, and many of the letters I get are from death row. I never thought I would be asked to be with an inmate when he was executed. But this was the second time. I'll tell you about the first time in a later chapter.

The thing that impressed me most about JD as an individual was his concern for the oppressed and the underdog. He spoke so much about the poor, the Blacks, the Hispanics, and the Native Americans that I thought JD was Black. I didn't know he was white until a couple of weeks before his execution, when a friend in Florida sent me a newspaper clipping. It didn't matter; it just surprised me. I committed to go there to be with a man I had never personally met and to be there with him before and during his execution, as his friend and minister.

I arranged for airfare so his wife and child could go see him one last time. They flew in from Ohio and were able to spend a few hours visiting with JD the week before he was executed. The visiting room for death row inmates was up near the front of the prison. The inmates are brought to a small cubicle and seated across from the visitor. The two are separated by glass and must speak to each other by phone. There is no chance for intimacy, and there is no contact.

Some death row inmates are allowed to visit in the chow hall on weekdays. Attorneys and ministers visit with death row inmates in still another area of the prison, back in the prison proper. The inmates are brought to the area handcuffed and are under surveillance by officers. This area is large enough for only about four or five visitors. It is possible here to shake hands with the inmate and to speak with a measure of privacy.

LIFE ON DEATH ROW

Michael Lambrix occupied the cell next to Raulerson. Michael said this about his arrival to death row:

> It was already dark when I entered the wing....No sooner did I hear the gate leading on the wing slam shut [than] I heard a voice calling "Cell six." I didn't realize that I was in cell six until suddenly an arm reached around with a rolled-up newspaper and banged on the bars of the cell—I was in cell six, and I had my first "phone call."
>
> Unlike the Hollywood version of being the new guy in prison, nobody called out "fresh fish" or taunted me in any way. The voice that called me quickly told me his name was JD (James D. Raulerson) and asked me what wing I came off—he thought I simply had a cell change. I told him I just came in and that my name was Mike.
>
> As I kicked the old newspapers and trash towards the front of the cell, JD talked to me. He held a mirror around the wall that separated our cells, so that I could see him—and I suppose, more importantly, he could see me. He asked me if I wanted a cup of coffee or anything. I thought he was joking...but a moment later he was reaching around the wall holding a steaming cup of hot coffee out for me. As I accepted that from him, a moment later he reached around again with a pack of cookies.
>
> As I hesitantly accepted the food, I told him I didn't have any money yet, and he laughed. I'll never forget what he told me—"Hey man, we're all in this together. Back

here, we look out for each other." Soon word got around the wing that a new guy was on the floor, and others hollered at me, each introducing themselves by whatever name they chose to be called, and more often than not, also asking me if I needed anything.

Within just a few hours, various others sent me an assortment of snacks, a bag of instant coffee, several cups and spoons, even a few bars of soap and a new bed sheet to throw over the moldy canvas-covered "mattress" that lay on the steel bunk.

...I was exhausted from the long day but too curious about my new world to want to sleep. Besides, the noise would not die down until after midnight, so I stood at the front of the cell and talked to JD for hours as he patiently told me about my new world.

J. D. Raulerson had already been on death row many years by the time I came in early 1984. He was an easy-going guy who called himself a "Christian Buddhist" and was self–educated in many vocations. I could not have asked for a better neighbor, as in the weeks and months that I adjusted to this new life, JD generously mentored me, never once asking for or expecting anything in return. But before the year was out the Governor signed his death warrant, and in January 1985, James D. Raulerson was executed.[2]

In that first year, there were eight men here on The Row put to death, one almost every month, and at a time when there was barely 100 of us here. That number now has increased to almost 400, with executions averaging two yearly.[3]

In 1979 John Spenkelink was the first inmate executed in Florida since execution was again legalized. His was a very controversial execution. JD was killed in January 1985, and Ted Bundy was put to death four years later in 1989.

A Handwriting Expert Comments

I never ask inmates about their crimes, or rather their convictions (some are innocent). I am always willing to listen to whatever they want to share. JD shared quite a bit in his letters. I recall that he had extremely unusual handwriting. When you read ten thousand inmate letters each year, you learn to spot handwriting quirks. JD made his (cursive) capital I's backward. This intrigued me, so much so that I had his handwriting analyzed by a professional handwriting expert. I purposely did not tell the woman that the handwriting belonged to an inmate. She knew nothing about him.

She told me that the way he made his I's indicated a parent relationship that was almost nonexistent. I never had much confidence in handwriting analysis, but as I learned more about JD, I found she was right on target. Of course, problems with parents would apply to most inmates. It is incredible how many people in prison come from homes where they had no real structure. Fragmented families produce fragmented people. It is fair to say that virtually all inmates come from fragmented families.

JD was given up at birth and raised by his grandmother, whom he thought was his mother. He never spoke of his father, and I'm not sure he ever knew him. My recollection is that his father was an alcoholic who did not want a child. At about age eleven, during another of the many arguments in his home, he overheard his stepfather yell, "Why don't you tell the boy you're not really his mother?" Those words pierced JD's young heart like a dagger and would prove to be words he would hear in his mind time and again.

He could not deal with the pain these words brought him. He ran away from home and was continually in trouble. The ensuing years found him in and out of juvenile homes and detention centers. His four brothers all had different homes, including Danny Miller, the brother JD loved and spoke of often. JD spent some of his young life searching for his "real" family. There was a point when his biological mother did come back into his life, but by that time he was a terribly confused and angry young man.

One of JD's closest loved ones was his Aunt Bonnie. She told me that JD was never really in a stable, loving situation. Life must certainly look different from the eyes of those raised in severely dysfunctional situations. It is difficult for the average person to know what the less fortunate deal with, and JD had a dysfunctional background, to be sure.

His Adopted Father Died in His Arms

His unfortunate teen years kept him in trouble with the police for things like petty theft. His search for an identity and a sense of belonging drove him from one city to another, and he wound up in Atlanta, where an older man, Dennis Raulerson, befriended JD and took him in as a son. They eventually moved to Ohio, where JD took the name of his adopted father. They opened a restaurant, and JD helped make the business successful. At last, his life had meaning and purpose. But then an event of incredible irony occurred.

In the darkest moment of JD's young life, his adopted father was shot and died in JD's arms during a 1973 robbery of the Raulerson restaurant—similar to the crime JD was executed for. Many who knew JD said that Dennis Raulerson's death pushed him backward. All the ground he had gained was lost and then some. It was a case of one step forward and two steps back. He had more confrontations with the law and settled into a life of crime that eventually led to his execution.

THE EXECUTION

When JD's wife, Alicia, went to visit, he was nearing his execution date and already under what is termed *deathwatch*. The inmate is moved from death row and placed in a somewhat secluded area of the prison where there are three or four cells. He is there until the time of his execution or until there is a stay, or perhaps clemency. He is watched by an officer stationed outside his cell so he does not commit suicide and cheat the state out of the execution. JD's cell was only a few feet away from the room with the electric chair.

I arrived in Jacksonville a few days before the execution. Before the execution, I went to the federal courthouse in Jacksonville and listened to the court's finding. UPI reported the finding:

> The Supreme Court refused today to halt the execution of James David Raulerson early Wednesday, but a second condemned killer got an indefinite reprieve from Florida's electric chair. The Court denied Mr. Raulerson a stay by a 6-to-2 vote, clearing the way for his execution at the Florida State Prison near Starke for killing a Jacksonville policeman in a 1975 robbery.[4]

I drove to Starke, about an hour from Jacksonville. After finding a motel and getting settled, I found JD's biological mother and brother Danny at another motel. It was not a very good motel, but it was the cheapest in town, again bearing out what is virtually always true—inmates' families are poor.

After some introductory talk and general discussion about

the event, I told JD's mother and brother that there was still some hope left, though I'm not sure anyone believed it. We discussed what time we would meet at the prison that night for their final family visit, and I prayed with them. I had a long sleepless night ahead of me, but my problem was nothing compared to theirs; I would lose sleep, but they would lose a brother and a son.

When it was getting dark outside, I left for the prison and met JD's mother and brother Danny at the front gate. As you drive into the parking lot, the execution chamber is visible. Florida State Prison is a pale green complex with a heaviness that hangs over it. There is an oppression you can almost feel. It is an ugly place in every respect.

I would spend the next twelve and a half hours in that prison. The darkness of the night seemed appropriate.

I spent the night outside of JD's cell and talked with him and the officer stationed there. That was a night I will not soon forget. Sometimes when I look back on all that takes place in an execution, it's difficult to keep tears from my eyes. It's not like anything else in life I have ever experienced. It is cold, calculated, and controversial. Whether or not you agree with the death penalty, you must agree that it is an event unlike any other human experience. I don't have anything with which to compare it. It's not like being at the bedside of someone who is dying or at the scene of a wreck where death is imminent. In my human experiences, it stands alone.

One former warden of the prison says that while he was once a proponent of the death penalty, the horrors of the executions have changed his mind. Ron McAndrew wrote:

> The flames that consumed Pedro Medina's head when the execution went seriously awry, the smoke, the putrid

odor, and his death by inferno is deeply embedded in my brain. The memory of telling the executioner to continue with the killing, despite the malfunctioning electric chair, and being at a point of no-return, plagues me still....

Searching my soul for answers that would satisfy the question on just why were we killing people and why our governor and politicians would do their "chest pounding" over these ghastly spectacles was difficult. I began to remember myself as the person who went to Florida State Prison with a firm belief in the death penalty. And even though I still professed this belief, the questions of why we were doing this and if it were necessary, would not leave my mind. While appalled by the physical act of tying a person to a chair and burning him to death, I did not deny the reasons for the act.

Here I want to say that one must be careful in searching his soul...one may just find that God is there and that He does not support the barbaric idea that man should execute man.[5]

I was not an activist when J. D. Raulerson was executed, and I'm still not. Several anti–death penalty groups were involved in trying to prevent his execution. That was not my reason for being there. The actual number of protesters was smaller than the number of police officers who gathered to show their support. I was told by people gathered outside that the moment was tense.

One lady told me, "You could really feel the tension. It was like two great enemies were fixed for battle. You could almost feel the vengeful hate from the police officers. The police were joking and laughing. The protesters were pretty much silent; some seemed to be praying."

I look back on that cold Florida night, and none of the

memories are pleasant. Seeing the bitterness build in JD's mother as it became obvious that her son was going to be executed is a vivid recollection. Perhaps she felt some of the blame. I'm certain many parents would feel that way even if they had been good parents. I'm sure she must have carried some heavy feelings of guilt into the visitation area, and even more as officers came to escort her out of the prison at midnight. Danny, another family friend, and I walked to the parking lot with her. She was frantic. She raised her fist toward the heavens and screamed out at God. Her heart was heavy with the weight of the event and perhaps the pain of the past.

Danny and I went back into the prison. The officers brought us to a small, secure area for a brief contact visit with JD. They strip-searched JD, and then they took Danny into a separate room and strip-searched him as well. I was patted down. The reason for the search was to check for drugs that could be used to either numb JD or enable him to overdose. Then the three of us sat around a small table with an officer close enough to listen in on the conversation.

I didn't have much to say. Danny and JD both tried to hold up and not show any pain, although I'm sure it would have been easier to hug each other and shed some tears. The time passed quickly, and soon Danny was led away. There was an obvious loss for words as the brothers separated for the last time. Danny turned one last time and forced a smile. JD looked at him and sort of nodded his head. He had not seen a whole lot of his brother at any time in their young lives, and he knew he would never see his brother in this world again. Danny wrote me a very nice note after the execution, thanking me for being there: "Guess you are like Coca-Cola. You are the real thing." I appreciated those words. I liked Danny.

JD was strip-searched again and handcuffed, and we were escorted back to the deathwatch area. JD was placed in his cell and strip-searched a final time. An officer was seated outside his cell, and a chair was placed there for me. It was about 12:45 a.m., and an uncomfortable situation for everyone.

I had been treated well by the Florida State Prison officials. Superintendent Richard Dugger and, I believe, Major Mathis were the men in charge of this execution. Earlier in the day, Superintendent Dugger invited me to his office and briefly explained the execution procedure. That's where I first met JD's lawyer, Stephen Bright, a man I genuinely liked.

The hours seemed to pass swiftly as the night worked its way toward 7 a.m. JD was not nervous. He had accepted Christ on death row a few years earlier. He knew his Bible well, and he knew that God would be faithful to His promises. He knew God would never leave him or forsake him (Deut. 31:6). JD believed the promise, as the apostle Paul said, "For to me, to live is Christ, and to die is gain," because "to be absent from the body [is] to be present with the Lord" (Phil. 1:21; 2 Cor. 5:8). He had a peace that only God could give. He didn't ask questions about what was going to happen after he died; he knew. He was saved, and he had within him the Holy Spirit of God comforting him and giving him strength.

What stands out to me is the concern JD still showed for others. He was writing some last-minute letters to people he loved and who had been friends during his confinement. He asked me to promise I would "get some rest after the ordeal is over."

I felt very confident about JD's relationship with God, through His Son, Jesus. I never had any doubts about him; he never gave me any reason to, and I witnessed the grace of God active and alive in his life during the execution ordeal. He was only thirty-three years old when he was executed.

About four o'clock, they brought his last meal to him. It was a pretty typical breakfast. He refused it and offered it to me. I also refused it, and JD asked the officer assigned to watch if he wanted it. He did.

We continued to talk about various things. I remember he put his pajamas on, as well as socks and a wool cap. I smiled and asked the purpose of the cap and socks. "It's the dampness in this place, in the walls and floor; you can catch cold real easy." He grinned and shrugged his shoulders as if to say, "You never know."

Not long after that, officers came to lead me away and make preparations for the execution. JD and I exchanged a few final words, said a short prayer, and shook hands through the bars. As I was being escorted out, just as I reached the turn in the hallway, he said, "Don, thanks for being here. I love you, man."

"I love you too, JD," I said as I turned the corner and followed the officers up a small set of stairs. They took me to the dining hall, where about twenty-five Jacksonville police officers and JD's attorney had gathered. The police officers had come to "enjoy" the execution; they were fellow officers of the man JD was convicted of killing. They served us coffee and fresh-baked breakfast rolls. It was a strange atmosphere.

Superintendent Dugger came through the area and mingled with everyone for a brief moment. He showed professionalism in every dealing I had with him.

Outside the prison, across the road, a large number of officers from all over Florida gathered. They sold and wore T-shirts that read "Raulerson, make my day!" There was also a small group of people gathered in opposition to the death penalty. I learned there was some harassment of death penalty protesters by police officers that cold January morning in 1985. Some of the police officers were talking loudly enough to be heard by the protesters across the way: "We have something to make a fire out of now," they said, speaking of the placards the protesters held. I also learned that the officers cheered when the hearse carrying JD's body drove by. However, inside the prison, I was unaware of any of these activities.

As I waited in the dining hall, JD was prepared for the execution. This included shaving his head and the back of his right calf to enhance the electrical contact. Florida inmates are generally dressed in blue pants and shirts. The men on death row had on orange T-shirts. JD was not clothed in blue or orange for the execution, however. He was wearing oversized white pants and a white shirt. The back of his right pants leg was split along the calf area just below the knee to allow placement of electrodes.

FACING THE ELECTRIC CHAIR

About 6:45 a.m., the command was given for us to follow officials down the hall and out the backside of the prison. As we walked to the back door, an eerie silence settled over the prison. There seemed to be no noise, almost like it was empty. Every inmate was aware of what was happening, so there was no stirring. We got into the waiting vehicles that would take us to the execution chamber. It was a short ride.

We filed into the witness box in no particular order and were seated in the three rows of chairs facing the execution chamber. I was seated in the front row, directly across from the electric chair. Had it not been for the glass partition, I could have touched JD. To my left was attorney Stephen Bright, and to my right, one of the Jacksonville officers.

It was a quiet and solemn crowd, though I recall a few comments, such as, "Well, we're finally getting the [expletive]." There were also a few tears, perhaps in memory of the slain officer, or perhaps because another human life was about to be taken. Almost immediately after we had all been seated, JD was brought into the chamber from a door at the back of the room. There was a small rectangular window in the wall next to the door, where a hooded executioner peered through the opening, awaiting the command from the superintendent to pull the switch. Also on the back wall was a phone where an officer stood awaiting a possible last-minute call from the governor's office, but no call came.

After JD was seated, he was strapped securely into the chair across the forehead, chest, arms, and legs. It wasn't for security but because it is a violent thing when electricity surges into the body. A metal cap was placed upon his head, and the wire from it was visible, as was the wire from the clamp attached to the back of his right calf.

Superintendent Dugger stood to JD's right with a microphone in his hand. Two doctors stood behind him with their white medical smocks and stethoscopes. A black veil was attached to the metal skullcap. The time had come. Heaviness covered the entire place. There was an eerie silence. Superintendent Dugger held the microphone to JD's mouth for his last words: "I am sorry you are made a murderer through the state, Mr. Dugger. James English killed Michael Stewart and used Stewart's gun to murder my cousin. I am sorry for you for taking my life. My family knows I love them and I love you."[6]

Just before the veil was dropped over JD's face, he looked

at me and his attorney and winked—that's right, he winked! I believe it was to let us know that the grace and peace of God were alive and active in his life, and he knew he would soon be in the presence of God. I witnessed a man die with peace and courage that only God could give. I'm not sure anyone else there that day viewed his death from that perspective. If they did, it was not obvious.

Superintendent Dugger turned to the executioner and issued the command to initiate the execution. In an instant, JD's hands—the only visible part of his body—went from a relaxed, open position to clenched fists that began to swell and turn blue, then purple. It looked as if they might burst. I don't recall the amount of time voltage surged through his body. It seemed much longer than it actually was.

After the electricity was turned off, the two doctors individually checked his heart and pronounced him dead. However, before they could get to him to make the death announcement official, he was already with Jesus!

One of the police officers went quickly to the door and waved his handkerchief to alert his comrades across the road that the convicted cop-killer was dead. There was an early morning fog and a damp coolness that seemed almost fitting for the moment. As I left the chamber, it seemed like there should be something else to do. There wasn't; it was over. However, as I often preach to inmates, "It ain't over when it's over if you know Jesus Christ!" And JD did! That is really my purpose in going into the prisons—not to get men and women out of prison but to get them into heaven.

My ministry is not an approval of crime. God forbid! Actually, it is an effort to prevent other crimes. I am not on the inmates' side and against the police. I am on the side of the law, but that does not mean I can't love inmates. I am on the side of the gospel. I want to see all people set free!

Was JD guilty? I guess we will never know this side of eternity. I do know with some assurance that he was saved. I am so grateful for God's amazing grace. I can also tell you with further assurance that I witnessed God being faithful to His Word. He promised never to leave or forsake us and to give us eternal life. He also promised that those to whom He gave eternal life would never perish. He promised to indwell believers and give a peace that passes understanding. I saw God be God in the darkest moment of a man's life.

Chapter 2

ALMOST EXECUTED: THOMAS GERALD LANEY

WHEN I MET Thomas Gerald Laney, he had been convicted of first-degree murder and was on death row in Tennessee. He is now serving a life sentence. He shared his story with me many years ago.

A GLIMPSE OF HELL

In Thomas Gerald Laney's own words:

> Don, I was shot all to pieces, laying in an emergency room in Kingsport, Tennessee. I saw myself raise up out of my body and begin to float toward the ceiling like a ghost. When I turned to look back, I saw my own bloody body and all the people working to save my life....I had tubes in my mouth and nose, and IVs were all over my body. I was really a mess.
>
> I floated right on through the ceiling and the roof. I could see air conditioner units on the roof and cars on the parking lot under the hospital lights. As I got higher, I could see the streetlights of Kingsport and the lights of cars as they moved along the Kingsport streets. I seemed to be moving faster as I got higher....I have vivid, candid memories of this experience...like it happened yesterday.
>
> At this point it was like something caught me and just sucked me into space like a vacuum. I was really moving fast, and I couldn't see anything behind me now....I zoomed right past the stars—what a beautiful sight to behold. My mind was filled with wonderment and an inner calm as I passed millions and millions of stars.
>
> I had no concept of time, but apparently all of this happened in a matter of minutes or maybe even seconds. I was afraid, but I didn't know what to do. Don, when I first shared this, I didn't think anyone would believe me. It really happened; you know I couldn't and wouldn't make up a story like this.

Almost Executed: Thomas Gerald Laney

I assured Gerald I believed him and related some similar stories I had encountered with others. However, all the accounts I had been exposed to were from Christians who had near-death out-of-the-body experiences. Gerald's story was quite the contrary.

In just an instant I was beyond the stars and into a darkness that is indescribable. I could see nothing, not even my hand I placed in front of my eyes. It was sort of a gummy darkness. I mean it was a darkness that you could feel. A tiny pinpoint of light soon came into view, and soon it began to glow. I was headed straight for it. Then something strange happened. I started falling, tumbling toward it. The closer I got, I could see it was actually a ball of fire and could even feel the heat from it. The flames leaped and sparks flew from the object. It was like an orange, glossy sea of fire.

Don, at that time, a terrible odor from the flames became obvious, an awful stench, the most awful smell I had ever encountered. It was like rotten eggs, a skunk, and sulfur combined, and then ten times worse. As the terrible odor intensified, I could hear hair-raising screams. I snapped [a prison term often used to mean suddenly understood]. This was people screaming. This odor was that of burning flesh. I was headed to hell. And, Don, I was almost there.

I remembered that my grandmother had always told me that if I didn't change my ways and quit my fast living I would someday wind up in hell. I also remembered how I justified my life of violence and crime. I would do like that thief on the cross I had heard about, live like I wanted, and just before I died, I would ask God to forgive me. My leather jacket, my Hawkbill knife, my gun, and my Harley were all I lived for. I thought I was Mr. Bad, and Mr. Bad wasn't afraid of nothing—but he was that night. That night, Mr. Bad was afraid! Maybe for the first time in my life, I was frightened.

The heat from the flames was burning me. I did not breathe because of the terrible stench. I tried to shut my eyes, but the sight remained. I didn't know what to do. I prayed, "God, please, please let me go back." I was dangling over the flames of hell. In an instant, suddenly I was spinning in reverse away from the flames. I was moving so fast, going back the same route I had come, back through the awesome stars and back into the view of Kingsport. I was moving so fast I thought I would surely splatter like a bug on the windshield as the roof of the hospital came into view. But I didn't. I floated very gently down and back into my body.

I remember as I came back through the ceiling, I could see my mother rubbing my arm and my father with his head down praying. My spirit, or soul, just eased right back into my body. I opened my eyes and saw my father. I screamed as loud as I possibly could, "Dad, get me out of here." I had never been afraid of anything in my life, but now I was scared to death. This experience should have literally scared the hell out of me, but it didn't. I was frightened, but I did not change.

LEARNING LESSONS

Gerald Laney awaited execution in Tennessee's electric chair. He told me, "I wouldn't be on death row if I had agreed to turn state's evidence on my gang members." It doesn't seem right. A man is either guilty and worthy of a death sentence based solely upon his crime, or he is not. It should be that simple. However, the way the US justice system works, it is not that simple.

There was never any doubt about Gerald Laney's guilt. If he

Almost Executed: Thomas Gerald Laney

is guilty of murder in the first degree, he should be sentenced based upon the crime, right? Wrong. In the case of this man, he was sentenced based upon his willingness to cooperate with law enforcement in gaining evidence on other people. He said, "The way it is, Don, is if you snitch on your friends, you live. Or you can be macho and die in the electric chair."

Gerald was born in Clinchco, Virginia, the son of a coal miner. His parents, Willie and Ida, remained by his side during his troubled and painful life. Gerald told me, "No telling how many tears I caused for my parents, but they always loved me. We were always poor, but at least in my early years we were very close."

Gerald's memories are mostly unpleasant. "My dad was a veteran and returned home from the war shell-shocked. He had also been injured working in the coal mines. The company he worked for owned the mines, the town, and the people that lived there. My troubled life didn't do anything to help my father. I was pretty hard to live with going into my teen years and for many years to follow. My dad, tired and suffering, tried to commit suicide by taking a large overdose of sleeping pills. Thank God he didn't die."

Gerald's father was eventually taken to the veterans' hospital in Johnson City, Tennessee. When it was obvious that he was going to be there for a while, Gerald's mom packed everything up and moved the family to Johnson City to be near Gerald's father. This was a big change in their family structure. His father then stayed home, and his mother found a job to support the family.

He said, "My life was confusing to me. From the third grade to being the national enforcer for the Ghost Riders motorcycle gang to here on death row, my life was one big jigsaw puzzle—with several missing pieces." Gerald told me of some disturbing events in his young life, things that most surely had a profound influence on his life of crime and violence. Gerald was often punished by his grade-school teachers because he could not keep up with the other students. It turns out he was dyslexic.

> I would have to stand in the corner with a dunce cap on, and other kids would make fun of me. I would have to stay in at recess while the other kids went out to play. I did the best I could. I tried, but I just couldn't read. My teacher would bend my hand back and slap it with a ruler. She would say, "Why can't you be smart like your sisters?" It would hurt me so bad. I would cry, but I just couldn't do it.

What a sad story. I wonder how many others have experienced unknowing or uncaring teachers or parents. How many others have gone through life with a disability without any help or understanding? Well, one thing is sure—the prison system is full of people like Gerald.

Gerald, like most of us, went where he was accepted. He was not accepted in school, but he was at the local pool hall.

> I used to go down there and look at all them bikes. I always liked those shiny motorcycles. Nobody made fun of me there. I guess that's why I kept going. That just sort of became a way of life for me. I was always there. Those bikers had a great influence in my teenage years. It was not a good influence, but I was feeling like a somebody when I was with them.
>
> Here I am, forty years old and on death row. Half of my life I have been locked up in prisons and juvenile homes. The other half has not been a whole lot of fun. I always

Almost Executed: Thomas Gerald Laney

felt like a nobody, and I guess that is one of the major reasons I wound up an outlaw biker. There, I was somebody. I couldn't read or write, but I could fight, and I could drink and do drugs, I could steal and rob. I could lie and cuss. I was somebody to a bunch of nobodies. Big deal, huh? It all seems so foolish now.

I can't pinpoint where it all started. I guess it was a combination of many things. My inability to learn due to my dyslexia was a big factor. Feeling rejected by others, by my peers. I'm not making excuses, Don, just trying to help you understand. I'm responsible for all of my actions. I can't say I didn't know what I was doing was wrong. It was mostly that I didn't care because it was doing something for my suffering ego. I always wanted to be a tough guy so people wouldn't make fun of me.

School was so threatening to me. I played hooky a lot and hung out at the pool hall. The owner would let me sweep up and empty trash cans in exchange for hanging out there. This was the hangout for the Ghost Riders motorcycle gang. I was really learning to admire them. People feared them because of their violent reputation. They always had money and girls and a type of respect. I wanted to be like them. I wanted to be one of them. This became school for me.

I was learning my lessons well. I learned to lie, steal, cheat, drink, cuss, do drugs, and sell drugs. I even started selling drugs for them at my school. Now I was getting some respect from my peers. Now I was somebody at school. It wasn't long though until I got into a fight with a teacher. I was no more than a foul-mouthed little punk. I got kicked out of school.

The day he got expelled was a happy one for Gerald. Now he didn't have to deal with the put-downs of school. He didn't have to hang his head and fake interest. He thought life would surely be better for him now. Gerald was through with the reading, writing, and arithmetic, and as he put it, "wheeling, stealing, and dealing" became his life.

HUSTLER

The Ghost Riders accepted me and gave me the name Hustler. That was my new identity and my pathway to Tennessee's death row.

I was involved in so much violence, I couldn't possibly tell about all of it. I'm not proud of any of it. However, at the time, I was. I always wanted to be somebody, and that made me feel important, at least to my gang members. One of the things I was most proud of during those early Ghost Rider days was bombing a Hell's Angels' clubhouse and motorcycle shop. I was proud of that.

Sitting here on death row, my mind often goes back, and I recall some of those painful memories, like clutching my right side in the back seat of my father's car, fading in and out of consciousness. I remember the blood seeping through my hands and my morphine-soaked brain making the passing cars appear as floating ships in a fog.

In the front seat of the car my parents were talking. Their words seemed to be in slow motion. They had just helped me escape from the hospital. They could have been arrested themselves and charged with aiding and abetting. You see, I was on parole and not supposed to be in North Carolina. Mother turned her head and spoke to me. Her words came to me like a tape being played at slow speed: "You nearly met your Maker this time, didn't you, Gerald?" Mother then turned to the map and helped Dad find the fastest way out of North Carolina.

My Maker? I wouldn't be foolish enough to blame my actions on anyone but me. Had I been stronger and wiser,

Almost Executed: Thomas Gerald Laney

I would have shot first. The other guy would be nursing his wounds, and I wouldn't be bleeding in the back seat of my father's car.

Well, this particular situation happened near Durham, North Carolina. There was a new Ghost Riders chapter up there, and they had invited us to come up for a party. The purpose of the party was to raise funds to help them find a clubhouse, to set up phone communications, and to increase involvement in illegal drug trafficking—just some of our worthwhile endeavors. Our entire membership got together and rode up the interstate for this big event in North Carolina.

As we got closer to Durham, we left the interstate and traveled on the back roads. We found the party location. There was a large field with a secluded valley, and that's where the party was going on. The decline was so steep we parked our bikes at the top of the knoll and walked down. However, I stayed at the top and sat on my bike. I examined the surroundings. I could see two pickup trucks parked side by side with the tailgates down to form a table.

Two large ice chests were full of cold cans of beer. Tables had been set up in horseshoe fashion around the trucks to resemble a bar. Spider and his old lady sat in the place of power, keeping an eye on everyone. Even from as far away as I was, I could see his sawed-off shotgun slung casually over his shoulder. As is typical, members were telling of their violent victories and destruction. It seems in these groups that the stories get bigger each time you hear them, and they probably were stretched quite a bit the first time they were told. The language you hear at these functions is not learned in Sunday school.

Not long after dark, the party was in full swing, most everyone was drunk, and the smell of marijuana was thick in the air. More than once I was offered a hit off of

27

someone's joint. The probates [men trying to earn their patches for membership] were being hassled quite a bit, having to bring drinks to the members on request.

It must have been about 9:30 or so when the sound of roaring motorcycle engines invaded the drunken air. Running to investigate, the Black Patches found fourteen members of the Hell's Angels. They came in on Harleys polished to the max. Instead of parking their bikes on the knoll, they rode down the steep incline. They rode right into the middle of our camp and demanded to know who the president was.

These were the same men I had heard so many stories about and whose clubhouse and motorcycle shop I had bombed. Raising my rifle, I told them we didn't party with Hell's Angels and would take it very kindly if they would leave. My men had gathered around me, raising their rifles and pulling their handguns. Then the obvious leader of the group stepped off of his bike and stared at me. "What's the matter? Why won't you boys let us party with you?" Then he spat a long stream of tobacco juice onto the ground and wiped his mouth with the back of his hand.

I was shouting more than talking: "We don't party with one percenters, with men who think they are better." It was all I could do to keep from shooting one of them.

It was silent for a moment, then one of them said, "We're not looking for trouble. We were invited to party with you."

I spun around and yelled to the crowd, "Who in the Ghost Riders invited a Hell's Angel to one of our parties?"

The man we called Creature said that he invited them because he wanted them to know that we were a peaceful chapter and would cause them no problems. Creature was president of the new North Carolina chapter.

I turned to [Spider] and asked, "What about this, Chief?"

Chief said, "Let them stay. Creature says he has partied with them before, and they are all right guys. Just have all of the Black Patches stay alert just in case."

This didn't make me feel very good, knowing I had bombed them, but if Chief and Creature were determined to have them stay, I could rest in knowing they didn't actually know who bombed them.

Quite a few bodies lay sprawled on the ground, passed and partied out. It was the early morning hours. Others were setting up their tents; some were already asleep in theirs. Chief and his old lady, Angel, were settled in and sleeping. I sneaked over to their tent and took out my knife. Kneeling down, I cut the ropes of support, and the tent came crashing down on them. You could hear laughter all through the valley. Chief came flying out of the tent, stark naked and in a rage. Cussing and swearing, he attempted to reset his fallen tent, insisting he would kill whoever did it.

One of our guys named Ferrari was sitting on the back of the pickup, talking to one of the Angels, a man they called Ace. Ferrari was trying to get one of the probates to go get him a beer. I offered to do it for him. I brought him the beer and said, "I'll even open it for you like they do at the club." I worked as a bouncer at the Pro-2 Club. Ferrari was surprised that I would do that, but I had seen the probate he was hassling crawl into the tent with a blonde, so I just did it, no big deal.

It didn't seem like a big deal at the time, but it was. When he told me, "Thanks, Hustler," the leader of the Hell's Angels began to stare at me. Ferrari and I had walked away from the fire, and I had asked him to lay off the probate for a while. When we went back, we saw the Hell's Angels gone and three full beers sitting there.

I spotted them huddled in a group and one of them pointing at me, nodding his head. That's when I first noticed that none of them were drunk. They had been sipping their beers. It was clear they were up to something, and I was the subject of their intentions.

I sought out all of our Black Patches and told them to keep a close eye on our guests, that something was in the wind. About an hour later, the two men that had been sitting on the pickup eased over to me, and [one of them] said, "You the one they call Hustler? What does that black patch mean? I've only spotted a couple of guys wearing them, and yours is the only one with a star in it." I now knew that they knew.

I lied about what the patch meant. The Hell's Angel pulled out a large hat pin and showed it to me. "I held a man down and gouged his eyes out with this hat pin." I played it cool and said the patch was for attending the most parties, that's all.

One of the Angels' probates came over to me and stood about six inches from my face. I assumed the others were goading him because he immediately began spouting off about how superior the Hell's Angels were. He raised his voice so everyone could hear, and since he was speaking directly to me, I said, "The only thing the Hell's Angels can do better is ride their bikes...IN THE DIRT!" I knew he was pushing for a fight, so I turned my back and walked off.

The rest of the night, there were Hell's Angels near me wherever I went. When daylight began to break, one of our members, named Dirty Bill, asked me to follow him up to his truck. He had a leather pouch to give me, and he had to leave the party early. Members were waking up and rolling up their bags. I wasn't that alert or I would have never gone up the hill alone. I placed the rifle I had

Almost Executed: Thomas Gerald Laney

been carrying in the weapons box and ignorantly walked up the hill with Dirty Bill and his old lady.

I took the pouch and walked up to some cars some of the old ladies had driven up in, and I tossed it in a car. I turned around, and there was the probate that had approached me earlier. I looked back to see Dirty Bill and Peaches; they were about 60 yards away and behind some cars, talking. The probate was holding a pistol, and the leader was about ten yards off to my left. I turned to look over the tops of the cars. I was alone. My life flashed before me. I knew death was close at my door.

The probate calmly walked up to me, placed the .38 to my chest, and pulled the trigger. The gun misfired! Fearing that the leader would shoot me, I grabbed the probate and threw him in between us. We fell to the ground and wrestled for possession of the gun. I kept thinking the leader was going to shoot me from behind, but I caught a glimpse of him, and he was in a Mexican standoff with Larky, one of our Black Patches. Attempting to get the gun away from the probate, a thunderous sound split the morning air. I had been shot!

He had pulled a derringer pistol from his boot. The pain in my right side was almost too much to bear. I was sure I was going to die. I was now in a rage, and adrenaline was pumping in me. If I was going to die, I wanted him to have something to remember me by. I grabbed his wrist and bent it backwards. He screamed in pain and dropped the derringer. I kicked it away. We struggled and rolled, trying to retrieve the gun. Suddenly I was on top of him. I bit down on his ear. I pushed on his face with my hands and pulled with my teeth. I ripped his ear off and spit it out.

He was screaming and crying in agony. I was bleeding and sure I was going to die. "You punk, I'm gonna kill you with my bare hands." I was now out of control and without any ability to reason.

I kicked him in the eye with my steel-toed boot. I probably would have killed him, but the leader swung his .357 Magnum toward me and yelled that his brother had had enough. I knocked his arm away, and as he swung the gun back toward me, he hit me in the face with the gun.

I grabbed his arm and wrestled him to the side of a car. "You gonna shoot me too?" I asked. He stared at me and looked down to my side and saw all of the blood, then he shook his head, no, and went over and picked up the derringer.

The probate was still on the ground, holding the side of his head and sobbing. All of the Ghost Riders and the rest of the Hell's Angels were now on the scene. I knew there would be no more shooting unless the Angels wanted to be massacred. Blood was also running down my chin where I had been struck with the pistol. I raised my shirt to examine the wound. I could see the powder burns and the black hole where the bullet entered my body.

The Angels had already drawn their guns when there was a distinct metallic click as Panama Red chambered a round into his .308. It was like a signal to the rest of the Ghost Riders, who readied their weapons. The Hell's Angels slowly put the guns away and gingerly helped the crying probate to his feet and to his bike. Panama Red told them to get on their bikes and ride and "take that sissy with you." They were outnumbered and they knew it.

One of the Ghost Riders named Germ helped me into his truck, and he and his old lady drove me away. One of the members from the new chapter led the way on his motorcycle. As Germ sped toward the hospital, his old lady cleaned my face and side as best she could. I only remember the sound of squealing tires as they raced to

Almost Executed: Thomas Gerald Laney

the hospital. I faded in and out of consciousness. I was sure I was going to die.

Two orderlies placed me on a stretcher and wheeled me into the emergency room. A nurse tried to cut my pants off of me, but they were my favorite leathers, so I got up and took them off. She was screaming at me to get back on the table. She begged me to lie down, fearful that I had internal bleeding. A doctor came in and gave me a spinal tap while IVs were being inserted. Before they could get me into the operating room, two Durham policemen came in to ask questions.

I lied to them and told them it was an accident. They said it didn't matter: "We have to investigate all gunshot wounds." I was on parole from the State of Florida and was not allowed to leave Tennessee. I looked on their shirts and could see they were city police officers. I got the idea of telling them it happened out of their jurisdiction, and I told them me and a buddy were out in the woods goofing off, and I was accidentally wounded. They told me the county sheriff would have to investigate, and they asked for my name.

I pretended to pass out, and I heard the nurse tell them they would have to come back later. I was then rushed to the operating room for a three-hour surgery. My appendix was removed because the bullet had passed through it. It was about 10 a.m. when they took me from surgery. I told the nurse I had to see Chief. When he came over to me, I insisted that he give me a gun.

"Are you crazy? You'll shoot a doctor or a nurse. I'm not giving you a gun."

I grabbed his shirt and pulled him close to me. "Look, this is Angels' territory. This is a death trap. They'll be checking all of the hospitals to find me."

He winked and slipped me a small derringer. Chief motioned for Tarp to come over and instructed him, "Stay

33

with Hustler. Make sure nobody gets to him, nobody!" By ten o'clock that night, all of the Ghost Riders had gone back to Tennessee.

The next morning, I called my parents to come get me. I explained that the hospital did not have my name, but the county police would be getting it real soon.

Dad said, "Me and your mother will be there as soon as possible." About one that afternoon, the three of us sneaked down the back stairs. I had seventeen metal stitches and tubes still hanging out of me. My plans did not include a hospital stay and a return to prison for parole violation.

Even though I was half-dead, my thoughts were of how this would help build my reputation as a tough guy, and I was thinking of revenge with a certain Hell's Angel probate. As my parents' Thunderbird raced back to Tennessee, I thought, "I beat the law again. I won't be going to prison for this." And I didn't, but I did make another trip [to prison] before I eventually wound up here on death row.

PROVING HIMSELF

Gerald had a reputation as a tough guy in the streets, but he had not proved himself in prison. He told me about a particular situation that did get the attention of the entire prison.

One day we were playing softball in the prison yard. Inmates were umpiring, and guards stood by to supervise. I was playing shortstop. This dude hit me a ground ball, I threw him out by at least ten feet, and the umpire called him safe. I went over to argue, and I was told by other inmates, "Let it go, man. Let it go." I was told the umpire was this man's punk, or girlfriend.

Guys told me, "Just forget it, man. Don't you know who he is?"

Almost Executed: Thomas Gerald Laney

"I don't care who he is. He was out, and he knows it."

The man who hit the ball pointed at me and said, "I'll make *you* my punk."

When the inning was over, I walked over to the dugout and got a bat. The man had not gone out to the field yet. When he turned around, I hit the guy in the face with my baseball bat. It broke his jaw and damaged his face pretty bad. Guards came and broke up everything, and I was put in the hole. While I was there, I learned that the man I hit ran the prison. I thought surely I would be killed, but rather, I had sort of a reputation built as a man you didn't mess with.

I spent four years in this prison. All it did was make me bigger, tougher, and meaner. I was Mr. Bad. That's right. Just ask me. I thought I was one of the toughest, meanest guys around. Yeah, I was Mr. Bad. Prison only made me worse. I got out and went straight back to my motorcycle gang.

I was really surprised at how large the gang had grown. It had seven chapters and over five hundred members. The old members knew how mean I was, and the new members saw how big I was. In only six months I became the national enforcer for the Ghost Riders. Now I was where I had always wanted to be. Big, tough, and bad. I can't tell you how much violence I have been involved with—beatings, stabbings, and shootings. My lifestyle was drugs, alcohol, hatred, violence, and massive destruction. Even my fellow gang members feared me. They knew there was nothing I wouldn't do. Little did I know or care that Tennessee had a cell waiting for me, and it would be located on death row.

It was October 16, 1980, when Gerald's death-row nightmare began. He was building a house, and his father was helping him with the construction. His father was a Christian and a lay preacher. Many nights he and his wife, Ida, had prayed and shed tears for Gerald, all to no avail to this point. On that fateful day, Mr. Laney tried to reason with Gerald about his lifestyle and the dangers that were in store for him.

Gerald told me:

> Brother Don, I was not used to anyone talking to me like he did. I was so filled with anger it didn't take much to set me off. He was only expressing concern that any father would have, but I didn't want to hear it. I pulled out my gun and stuck it in my father's face. I screamed at him, "Old man, one day you are going to push me too far, and I'm going to end it all for you." I told him I was going to leave for a while, and he had better not be there when I came back.

Gerald's father had been praying about how to reach his son. He told him that if he left the house at that time, he would not be back and that God would put him in a place where he would have to listen.

> I didn't listen to my dad. I didn't listen to nobody. It didn't even bother me that I had threatened to kill my father. I was almost always numb from drugs or alcohol or both.
>
> I went on into town to a bar that the Ghost Riders owned. One of the members asked if I wanted to make some extra money. I had been taking some LSD, and I was beginning to feel it. I was already drunk on beer. They wanted me to go to Kingsport and collect some money that was owed to them on a drug deal. It all seemed pretty simple.
>
> Without my knowledge, the gang member called the guy and told him I was coming and that he had better have the money for me or else. When the man came

Almost Executed: Thomas Gerald Laney

home, I was waiting for him in the shadows by his carport. As he unfolded, getting out of the car, I was surprised to see how big he was. I decided that I would try to ask him for the money rather than try a violent approach. I put my gun back in my belt and approached him.

This was not my style, but the guy was big, and I thought it was smarter to not have a big fight and attract attention. However, when I stepped out of the shadows, he pulled a gun and started shooting me. I pulled my gun and shot back. We both were hit. I fell face down, and the last thing I recall is thinking I was going to drown in my own blood.

It was about 2:30 in the morning when Mr. Laney's doorbell rang. He remembered the events of the day and his last words to Gerald, and he knew it was not going to be good news. A captain from the sheriff's department was at the door, and he told Mr. Laney that he had better sit down. He asked if he had a son named Gerald who had blond hair and a black beard.

Mr. Laney asked, "What has happened? What's wrong with Gerald?"

The captain told him that Gerald had been shot, and there was a good chance that Gerald was dead.

Mr. Laney was in shock. "Who shot him?" he demanded.

The captain told him that Gerald was shot by the man he had shot and killed.

"Oh my God, my God in heaven!" Mr. Laney yelled. He then asked where Gerald was.

The captain offered to drive Mr. Laney to the hospital, but he said he would go alone. When Mr. Laney arrived, one of the doctors who had worked on Gerald was coming out of the room. He told Mr. Laney that he and two other doctors had done all they could do. He told him he didn't think Gerald would make it, and if he did, it would be a miracle. Even then, the doctor said, he would be no more than a vegetable. But Gerald's dad believed in miracles, and he prayed for his healing. This was when Gerald had his near-death experience, where he felt himself almost in hell.

Time passed, and doctors still offered little hope, even though Gerald was clinging to life and to hope. He didn't recall what happened. He thought he had been in a bad car wreck. Weeks passed, and Gerald was told he would be paralyzed from the waist down and not have control of his bowels. He was told he would have to wear a diaper. Mr. Bad, in a diaper.

I lay back on my pillow and looked at my 110-pound body and all of the tubes sticking out of me. I couldn't believe what had happened!

I finally went to trial. It began on a Monday and was over by Friday. The only people who testified on my behalf were a sister and a doctor who testified that I was borderline retarded. It only took the jury an hour and a half to come back with the verdict: death by electrocution. My father was not in the courtroom for the verdict. I guess he felt it was more than he could take. At this time, I was able to walk, but now I wondered, What for?

I was led from the courtroom, handcuffed and shackled. When a trial like mine is finished, it is finished. Late that night, I was loaded up and driven to death row in Nashville at the Tennessee State Prison. As the heavy steel door creaked open, a glimmer of light shined on me and the two officers that accompanied me. The state guards told one of the officers to take my belongings, which were in a paper bag, and search them. They told the other deputy to take my chains off. The deputy wouldn't do it. He said I was too dangerous.

They took me to cell nine on walk three, and once

inside they took my chains off and told the deputies to leave, that they would take it from here. One of the deputies said, "Take it easy, Laney."

Yeah, I thought, take it easy. I'm still recovering from gunshot wounds, I'm barely twenty-eight years old, and I'm in prison for the third time and under the sentence of death. Yeah, take it easy, Laney.

I had not been on the row but a few days when a man came to visit. It was night, and the guards knew him well enough to let him on the walk and close the door behind him. He stopped at each cell and talked to each man, some longer than others. He didn't seem to be pushing himself on the guys. He just gave them an ear and asked if they needed anything. I even heard him praying with a few of the men. I knew he would be at my cell in a few minutes. Just what I needed in my life right now, a Jesus freak. I didn't want to be too rude and cause friction with the other inmates, but I told him we had nothing to talk about.

He caught me off guard when he said, "That's OK. I'll drop by on my next visit, and if you need anything, let me know." God had no place in my life, and I had nothing to talk to this guy about. What could a Jesus freak do for a man on death row?

THOUGHTS OF SUICIDE

The man's name is Frank Bainbridge, and he was a volunteer at the prison. Frank is a lay deacon in the Catholic Church and genuinely loves Jesus. Anyone who knows Frank knows he is born again and is interested in others being saved as well. Frank was actively involved in ministering to the men on Tennessee's death row for many years.

Gerald was not well. He had not recovered from the shooting. His leg was not healing and was getting worse.

DEATH ROW REDEMPTION

Gerald was ripe for demons to claim his troubled soul and broken body. They began to move in. Thoughts of suicide came; reasons for not living were abundant. He ran them over and over in his mind.

I thought about all of the people I had hurt, and all of the crazy things I had done. I knew I would be a burden to my family, so I decided on suicide. My leg hurt constantly. Big red sores popped out all over my leg. I hurt in every way. The doctor told me if my leg got worse, it would have to be amputated.

I didn't even know what the word meant. I said, "Does that mean cut my leg off?" The doctor nodded yes.

Later that night I took my sheets and made a noose. I didn't want to live. I planned my suicide, but that night I went to sleep with intentions of doing it the next day.

The next morning was Sunday. There was simply no light at the end of my dark, dark tunnel. I turned on my little TV, and while I waited for the ball game to come on, some preacher was on TV preaching. He caught my attention. He even said to have faith in God, and to demonstrate it to put my hand on the TV screen. I don't know why I did. I guess when you are desperate you do those things. Maybe God had me, finally, where I was desperate enough to reach out to Him. I don't know. I just did it. It felt like electricity running through my body as I prayed the sinner's prayer for the first time. I felt the power of God.

I knew something had happened in my life. I didn't know exactly what or how to explain it or who to tell it to, but something had happened.

Frank Bainbridge came by like he always did, and he said, "Gerald, I notice you are standing on that leg, and you look like you are gaining a little weight. How are you

Almost Executed: Thomas Gerald Laney

feeling?" He went to ask if there was anything he could do for me.

Gerald had experienced the life-changing power of Jesus Christ. He had received grace that many of us cannot even comprehend. Why would God love someone like Gerald? No, not *why*. Rather, how could God love someone like Gerald? He never stops loving us! He *never* stops loving us. He loves us unconditionally. We cannot do anything to make Him love us more, but neither can we do anything to make Him love us less. *God is love.* What an amazing thing that God is able to look beyond our faults and see our needs.

Frank knew something had happened. It showed in Gerald's very countenance. Gerald said, "I don't know how to read or write, and I can't talk very good, but I want to tell you something I've never told anyone else, and I don't want you to laugh at me. Besides that, I couldn't make up something like what I'm about to tell you."

Frank assured Gerald that he would not laugh. Gerald began to relate the out-of-body experience he had while in the hospital. He told it with excitement. Then he shared with Frank about placing his hand on the TV and praying the sinner's prayer. There was no doubt that his leg was healed, and there was no doubt that something had happened to Gerald that changed his whole being from the inside out.

Frank told Gerald that his was the most amazing testimony he had ever heard. He told him when he came back, they would discuss it some more and see what God wanted to do with Gerald's life.

After Frank left, I really felt a peace, but I couldn't see how God could love me, or more so, how I could possibly serve Him. I couldn't read or write; they said I was borderline retarded. My father had told me I had caused him more trouble than all nine of my brothers and sisters combined. I knew all of my failures, and yet, somehow, I knew He loved me. I knew this was real.

Gerald began to crusade for young people to finish school, and then one day he received news that his sentence had been vacated. His sentence was changed from death by electrocution to life in prison. Gerald told me with great passion:

I am unworthy of God's love and mercy. I came to prison a broken, crippled man, I had lost my health and my strength. I could not read or write. I was nothing and I had nothing, but I cried out to Him and He heard me. He saved me. It just shows that God's mercy is extended to everyone. Many times I wonder how He could love me. Yet I know from deep in my heart that He does love me! He loves me, and He has given me back my life. I will live for Him regardless. I believe God knew that I am serious about serving Him. Now He has given me back my life. I love Him and I praise Him!

Chapter 3

TEXAS-SIZED FORGIVENESS: ARNOLD MUNOZ

ONE OF THE most incredible stories I've ever heard comes from a Texas prison known as Eastham Unit until it was renamed in 2021. *Newsweek* magazine once called the prison America's toughest prison.[1] I don't know if that is true. At one time it was. I recall stories from inmates and officers before the federal courts ruled in an inmate's lawsuit against the state. They told about coming in from the fields and having to strip down and run through a line of officers who would beat them with belts as they ran through the gym to the showers.

The Texas system had inmates called building tenders who would beat other inmates at the officers' instructions. I knew a couple of the building tenders; they hated what they did, but they got special privileges. It was a brutal system. Gangs were also becoming a problem.

In 1972 inmate David Ruiz sued William Estelle, the director of the Texas Department of Corrections, over the living and working conditions, claiming the management of Texas prisons constituted cruel and unusual punishment, which is prohibited by the US Constitution's Eighth Amendment. The class action lawsuit brought to light problems that included overcrowding, poor security (resulting in the use of building tenders), inadequate healthcare, unsafe working conditions, and harsh and arbitrary discipline. The ruling resulted in significant changes in the Texas prison system over the next few decades.[2]

The Eastham prison was ironically my favorite prison to go to and preach in the chapel. They had some good services there. The chapel was always packed, and not because it was air-conditioned—it was like an oven in that chapel. I saw incredible things in that chapel, like what happened with Arnold Munoz and Raul Rodriguez, the man who killed Munoz's sister. I asked Arnold to tell his story.

Texas-Sized Forgiveness: Arnold Munoz

SHAKING THE HAND THAT KILLED MY SISTER

As I begin this testimony, I want to thank my Lord and Savior Jesus Christ for giving me a new heart, for taking the heart of stone out of me and putting in me a heart with love and compassion. I thank Him for giving me a heart that allowed me to love and forgive the man who killed my sister. My name is Arnold Munoz, and I'm a convicted murderer. At the time of this testimony, I am thirty-eight years old and have already spent sixteen years of my life in prison.

I don't know why I have this violent nature—sometimes I think it was the violence I experienced as a child that led to my violent nature. But if that is the case, then why do my brothers and sisters not have the same violent nature I have? When I look back on my life, I realize that I didn't believe in God. I didn't have God in my life. The violence that I speak about was the severe beatings my stepfather would inflict on my mother. Several times he stabbed her, once he broke her ribs—I also saw my mother stab him on several occasions. I saw my stepfather get into several knife fights. I saw him get stabbed. I also saw him stab several men. He was shot to death when I was seventeen years old.

The first thing that came to mind when he was shot to death was, "I have to get even." It took me two years to find the man that killed him. At that time, I killed two men and wounded another one during the shooting. For that crime, I got sentenced to twenty-five years in the Texas Department of Criminal Justice, of which I served eleven years. While I was serving time on that sentence, I was notified that one of my younger sisters had been shot to death; that was in 1980. I promised that I would get even with the man that killed her, and I would look forward to the day I would get the revenge. "One day, one day," I would say to myself. "One day I will get my revenge."

In the meantime I had so much hatred for this man that the only way I could vent this hatred was to pick a fight with someone else. I picked a fight with another inmate, and I stabbed him. In 1983 I was released from prison. When I was released, I had the attitude that I could do anything on the streets. I had a good education, a fast car. I had a good job. I figured the sky was the limit. I was one that always wanted women and money. I wasn't rich, but I had enough money to do the things I wanted, at least what I thought was fun at the time.

I stayed out of prison three years. At that time, I didn't believe in God, and I would have nothing to do with anybody that did believe in God. When anybody would talk to me about God, I would rebel. I believed the thought of God was a fantasy, something that the government had put out to keep the poor people oppressed. I just wouldn't believe. I didn't want to believe in God.

One day I called out to God. I don't know why, as like I said, I didn't believe in Him. I just stood there on the Harbor Bridge looking out at the water, and I said, "Lord, I've got everything I ever wanted, but I'm not happy. If You exist, God, would You show Yourself to me? Just show me, Lord, if You exist." I forgot about that prayer as the day passed on. I went on home, and about seven o'clock that night this friend of mine that was in prison with me came by. He had turned his life over to Jesus Christ.

He came in, and he told me these words: "Brother, God heard your prayer, and He sent me to talk to you."

I got chills all over my body because I remembered that I had prayed to God earlier that day. But still I was so imprisoned by things of the world that I told him, "Man, I don't believe in God. God is a myth. There is no such thing as God and Jesus Christ and the devil; that's a myth."

Texas-Sized Forgiveness: Arnold Munoz

This brother looked at me and said, "Brother, God told me to tell you that there is a battle for your soul. And God wants you to know that if you don't turn your life over to Him now, you will [end up] in a situation where you will turn your life over to Him."

I said, "I don't believe that." I just couldn't believe. I thought it was a fantasy. A few months later, when I was convicted of the murder that I am serving time for now, I remembered that man told me that I was going to be in a position where I would turn my life over to God. But still I thought I could get myself out of whatever situation I got myself in, and I still didn't want to call on God. When I received this life sentence, I just couldn't call on Him.

I remembered something my mother told me while I was in the county jail that made me start searching for the Lord. She said, "Son, you are killing me. Every time you hurt somebody, you are doing it to me. Call on God, and He'll change you."

I wanted to call on God, but I had such hatred for the man that killed my sister, and that had been seven years ago. But I still had such hatred in my heart for this man. Now that I was serving a life sentence, I figured I had nothing to lose. I said, "This man is in prison. I am in prison. I'll get my revenge, then I'll turn my life over to God." I even asked the prison administrators to send me to the Eastham Unit—the man who killed my sister was at Eastham.

The prison officials looked at my record and said I could not go to Eastham because the man who killed my sister was there. Later, I tried about two or three times to get transferred to Eastham, but they would not allow it. So I said to myself, "I'm doing a life sentence. He's doing a life sentence. Sooner or later I will meet up with him. In the meantime, I need to start calling on God." It surprised me that every time I called on Him—every time—He answered my prayer.

I remember one time down on the Retrieve Unit, I had gotten into an argument with another inmate. The first thing that came to my mind was that I had to kill him before he killed me. I went to my cell and got my knife and put it in my waistband. I was standing in my cell, waiting for the cell doors to open, and I remembered what my mother had told me in the county jail. I knelt down, and I said, "Lord, this is it. I don't want to hurt anybody anymore. Help me, Lord. I know You are there. I know You are listening to me. Just help me, Lord. Come to me. Don't let me do this. You know what I am capable of doing, Lord."

I don't know what else I told Him, but I know I prayed to Him. I could hear the other cell doors open and the inmates going out of their cells. I said, "Lord, don't let this cell door open." My cell door didn't open! I looked over toward my bunk, and I saw my Bible lying on the bunk. I went and lay down and hugged my Bible. I started crying, "Thank You, God, for not letting that cell door open."

The next day I got up and went and threw my knife away. I never saw the man I had the argument with again. I don't know what happened to him. I know that no one knew I had this problem with him—just this man, me, and the Lord. The only conclusion was that my God had come and solved the problem for me!

Then I started to walk with the Lord. I had this desire to walk with Him and to do the right things for His glory. Sometime later I had been transferred to the Ramsey I Unit, and I remember praying, "Lord, I want to follow You, but I don't know if I'm for real. I don't know what would happen if I'm tested. If I'm backed into a corner, Lord, I don't know what I will do. I want You to test me. Try my heart, Lord. See if I am for real. That's the only way I will know how sincere I am."

A short while later I was working in the fields. It was a

Texas-Sized Forgiveness: Arnold Munoz

hot day, and the wind was blowing. I heard this voice. It was clear, a clear voice that said, "You are going to shake the hand that killed your sister."

I looked up into the sky. I felt so small. I knew that without a doubt God was calling me for what He wanted me to do. I said, "Lord, I can do it. I will do it, but first, Lord, let me get this revenge that I have been seeking for so long, and then, Lord, I will turn my life over to You."

That voice persisted—at work, at school, even in my dreams, I would hear the voice, "You will shake the hand that killed your sister."

Finally, I could not resist the call. I said, "Lord, do whatever You want with that. If You want me to shake that man's hand, then make a way for us to meet."

But in my heart I said I had fooled God. I knew my prison record said that I could not go to Eastham. I was mistaken. I was not fooling God. Within a week I had been transferred to the Eastham Unit. I knelt and I prayed with tears in my eyes. I cried and said, "Lord, I have never been through anything like this. I don't know if I will respond or just react with this man. Help me, Lord. You are going to have to help me."

I arrived at the Eastham Unit on Thursday, September 8, 1988. I remember I could feel two presences walking with me all that Thursday and on Friday. One presence was that of the Lord Jesus Christ, reminding me to be patient and encouraging me that everything would be fine. The other presence was Satan, telling me to get even—that I had waited so long for this revenge that I had to get even.

On Saturday, September 10, at nine o'clock in the morning, I went to church. The chaplain asked if there were any men who had come from another unit. I stood up and said, "God has brought me to Eastham to change my heart of stone and give me a heart of flesh."

The congregation looked at me like I must be crazy.

49

At ten o'clock that morning I was invited to a Spanish choir practice session. When I went into that chapel at ten o'clock, I knew instantly that the man who killed my sister was in the chapel. Even though I had never seen him and did not know him, there was an evil presence— Satan was there! When I saw this man, he was directing the choir. I sat behind him. His back was to me. I felt Satan's presence so strong. I had so much hatred for this man. All this hatred I had for all these years was about to burst out. I remember I could see my sister lying in a puddle of blood, and I could imagine my mother crying over my sister. Satan was telling me, "You must get even."

I was crying. I wanted this revenge. But then I remembered that my God had brought me to Eastham to change my heart. I started praying and crying, "I can't do it, Lord. Help me. I can't do it without You." At that very moment, I felt the presence of Satan leave! I felt a peace and joy come over me that I had never felt before. I felt as if my God had hugged me and as if Jesus had His arms around me and was telling me to forgive. He was right there with me! There is no doubt in my mind that He was right there with me.

Then I looked at this man, and I didn't hate him anymore. I realized that I had love and compassion for the man. I wanted to get up and hug him and tell him to forgive me. I was confused, and I said, "God, what do I do now?" I felt as if Jesus was leading me by the hand. I got up, and I tapped him on the shoulder. I said, "I have got to talk to you right now."

The man turned and said, "I'm busy."

Then I said, "God wants me to talk to you right now."

We walked to the middle of the aisle, and I looked at him and said, "God brought me to Eastham for a purpose. He told me I was going to do something, and what He told me to do is about to happen. I am going to be obedient. I have to be obedient."

He looked at me with surprise in his eyes.

I told him, "Brother, God told me I was going to shake the hand that killed my sister." Then I shook his hand. I started crying because I had done something that I thought I would never be capable of doing. I hugged him, and I cried in his ear, "Brother, forgive me for all of the times I thought about killing you." We cried, we hugged each other, and we asked each other's forgiveness.

CHANGING THE HEART OF STONE

I know that my God was there with me. Even now as I share this, I feel His presence, and I know He is with me now. A few weeks later my mother came to visit me and my brother in Christ. I remember the words that she told him. She said, "Son, you might have killed my daughter, but now you are my son and your wife is my daughter. God has given me a larger family." She hugged him and kissed him. Here is this woman who had stabbed several men, and she had been stabbed. Here was a lady who always had to get her revenge, and she was hugging the man, forgiving the man that killed her daughter. God had done a miracle!

Now the relationship between this man and me is stronger than the relationship with my natural brothers and sisters. It is a relationship that God has made. This is something that cannot be destroyed. God knows that I have no hatred toward this man or his family, and I know that he has no hatred for me or my family. When I think of what God has done, how He changed my heart of stone, a scripture comes to my mind. In Ezekiel 36:26 the Lord says that He will take out the heart of stone and give us a heart of flesh. He gives us a new spirit. Another scripture says whenever you pray, to forgive, to ask God to forgive us. And I know that on September 10, 1988, God removed my heart of stone and gave me a heart of flesh. He made us one. He made me, my mother, and the man who killed my sister one in Him.

I am serving a life sentence, and the courts say I will never get out, but brothers, it doesn't matter anymore. It doesn't bother me that I am serving this life sentence. I have seen what the Lord has done in my life and in the lives of others, and I pray He continues to use me to bring others to Him. If I must be here the rest of my life, I know He will be with me. I've got no reason to worry.

Before I close this testimony, if there is anybody that you need to forgive, you must forgive them. I know it is difficult, but with the help of Jesus Christ, you can do it. He will give you the courage to do it. Satan told me I couldn't forgive, my friends told me I couldn't forgive, and I told myself I couldn't forgive. But God said, "Son, you can forgive." I thank my Lord Jesus Christ for saving me and for saving my mother. I pray that this testimony will help bring others into the kingdom. I love you, and I want you to know my Jesus.

Arnold reached out to God, and God heard his prayer. He prayed a prayer similar to the one below. Everyone who is saved prayed this kind of prayer:

Come into my heart, Lord Jesus, and save my soul. I am a sinner. I need You as my Savior. I believe You are the risen, living Son of God. I confess that I cannot make it to heaven without You. Thank You for saving me. Amen.

When I first met Arnold, he told me of his craving for revenge. He told me of his stepfather taking him to bars and clubs when he was very small, telling him to stay outside, where Arnold would throw punches with the other kids. Even though

Texas-Sized Forgiveness: Arnold Munoz

he said they were just playing around, I imagine it made him tough.

I actually went to Corpus Christi to meet his mom and pray with her. She had so much hurt in her life, but Arnold was able to win his mom to Christ.

While I was there, I went to the little bar where Arnold would pass the time roughhousing with the other kids. I could visualize a little boy standing around that front door, learning to be tough. Thank God for His mercy and grace.

Here ya go
preacher

Don Dickerman
Box 575
Hurst, Texas 76053

Chapter 4

"THE MEANEST GUY IN PRISON":
JIM CAVANAGH

Don Dickerman with Jim Cavanagh (left)

I JUST GOT OFF the phone with Jim. I met him through a Canadian former inmate named Ernie Hollands, whom I met when I was a guest on *100 Huntley Street*, a popular Christian talk show in Toronto. Ernie Hollands, once a bank robber but now a Christian, was also a guest on the show.

Ernie was a well-known bank robber in Canada. He spent twenty-five years in some of the same prisons as Jim Cavanagh, but they did not grow up together. Makes me think Nova Scotia might be a tough place to grow up. Hollands said his mother was a thief and taught him to steal.

> I remember when I was eight years old, she would take me shopping with her and show me what to steal. "Go ahead, put that lipstick in your pocket or get that perfume." I learned to steal from my mom.
>
> My dad would tell me when I got home what a good job I had done. All they would do is drink and fight and tell me what a problem I was. Not once did they tell me

"The Meanest Guy in Prison": Jim Cavanagh

they loved me. Before I was even a teenager, they sent me to a juvenile detention center. They never came to visit.

Ernie described some of the "unthinkable abuse" that occurred in the juvenile facilities that made him feel "like the lowest thing alive." He managed to escape and go back home.

I knocked on my home's door, and my father came to the door. "You never came to see me. I thought I'd come see you."

He wouldn't let me in and said, "You don't live here anymore. You can't come in. You're a big boy now. Go take care of yourself."

I don't even know how to explain how I felt. I was so angry at life and didn't understand why it was like this.

So I took to the streets, using my stealing skills taught by my mom and the hardheartedness I had learned from my dad. I burglarized homes, robbed stores, and didn't care about anybody. Why should I? No one cared about me. I stole a pistol in one of the home burglaries in California. I slept in box cars and on the streets. I would vow to be the respected outlaw. I had a gun and began to rob stores. I would be the toughest of them all. I began to rob banks. I was making headlines as a bank robber. It got me twenty-five years in prison— from Millhaven to Kingston Penitentiary to Collins Bay. I escaped five times.

I talked to Ernie after the show and told him I'd like to minister in Canadian prisons. He gave me the name to contact in Kingston. Jimmy Cavanagh, a notorious former inmate, was now the director of Prison Fellowship in Kingston. Ernie said he had been in all seven of the Kingston prisons. I didn't even know there were seven prisons in Kingston, but I have been in all of them now.

RESTORATION

Jim Cavanagh had a troubled childhood. He was sent to a school for troubled boys when he was ten, but because of the abuse he experienced, he continually ran away. When he was fifteen, he asked a judge to send him to an adult prison so he could escape the abuse at the school. Canadian federal prisons became Jim's home for twenty years, and he was once called "the meanest guy in prison."[1]

I recall an instance of the brutality of prison he shared with me. He told of a young inmate coming in as a new inmate and the fear in this young man's eyes. Another inmate approached the young inmate and said to the boy, "You are mine, boy." Jim said this infuriated him, and he told him, "If you touch that boy, I will kill you!"

> I heard he had abused the boy, and I went to the man's cell and told him, "I told you if you touched that boy, I would kill you. I'm going to my cell and get my knife, then I'm coming back to kill you!" [This, of course, was before Jim was saved.] He had a knife, and I had a knife. We wrestled around in the hallway, and I killed him. That's the way I was. I knew the pain of sexual abuse. You know, Don, when he died, I felt something come into me, like it left him and entered me.

Jim had escaped from many prisons. He learned to open handcuffs with a homemade paper clip—he even showed me how to do it. He would fake an emergency that required a hospital visit and hide the paper clip in his mouth. While in the back seat of the car, he would cough up the paper clip, undo his cuffs, commandeer the car, and escape.

However, while Jim was in Millhaven prison, his friend Ernie Hollands sent him a letter urging him to accept Christ. Through an encounter with the Lord in prayer, Jim's heart was captured by Christ's love. What a dramatic change!

Then Jim had a real emergency and was paralyzed by a ruptured blood vessel in his spinal cord. Even though the doctors told him he would never walk again, Jim's prayer was, "Lord, restore me."[2]

At Collins Bay, a prison known for so much violence it was dubbed Gladiator School, Jim went to the exercise yard in his wheelchair. He was talking to an inmate known as Meathead. Jim asked how far it was to walk around the track, and Meathead said, "I think it's 440 yards."

Jim said, "Someday I'm gonna walk all the way around it."

> I heard a voice say, "Why not now?"
> I answered from my inner man, "Yeah, why not now?"
> I put my feet out of the wheelchair, and with all my strength I stood to my feet. Much of the way I leaned on the wall, but slowly, one step at a time, I made my way around the yard. It took me over an hour, but, Don, when I made it, the whole prison was cheering for me.

Jim, who now walks with two canes, was released from prison in 1983. Then, in 1989, he became the Prison Fellowship chapter director in Kingston, ministering in the prisons where he was once an inmate. Speaking of the changes in his life because of his faith in Jesus, Jim said, "It was an inner healing I received, and I felt free inside. I didn't have to try and escape anymore; I was already free. I was able to forgive myself and have love and appreciation for myself. And then God enabled me to love my fellow prisoners and have forgiveness toward them whenever they would do something to offend me. God is bringing about an internal change, and with that internal change is external evidence."[3]

Here ya go
preacher

Don Dickerman
Box 575
Hurst, Texas 76053

NORTH BAY, CA 949
PM
1 A
23 JUN
1988

Chapter 5

REAL DEMON POSSESSION: DAVID BERKOWITZ

Don Dickerman visiting with David Berkowitz

I HAD BEEN GOING to Texas prisons for a few years to preach, and like most of the nation, I had heard about the man called the Son of Sam. I heard on the news that he had been caught, was sentenced to more than 350 years in prison, and had been sent to Attica prison. I wrote him a letter that basically said, "David, God still loves you, and Jesus can save you." He wrote me right back and said, "If I get out of here, I'll kill you!" That ended our correspondence.

In 1976 and 1977 New York City was terrorized by a series of satanic murders. The entire nation was in shock over the bizarre occult crimes, which killed six and wounded seven, attributed to the Son of Sam. David Berkowitz was arrested and pleaded guilty to the historic crime spree. The so-called Son of Sam crimes are still among the most infamous in New York history.

Ten years after he said he would kill me if he got out, I was preaching at Sullivan Prison in Fallsburg, New York, where David was incarcerated at the time. I didn't know he was there and didn't even know what he looked like. After I preached that night, an inmate came forward and put his arm around me, gave me a firm hug, and extended his hand. He said, "My name is David Berkowitz, and I want you to know I appreciate you coming into these dark places with the light of the gospel, and I appreciated the service tonight."

I said, "David, are you saved? When did you accept Christ?"

He told me he was saved a couple of years earlier at the Clinton prison in Dannemora, in upstate New York. I have been there. I asked David if people on the outside knew about his conversion. He said, "Not really. I'm not sure I'm ready to deal with all of that."

I understood what he was saying. He had not spoken to the news media for sixteen years. I said, "David, if you ever want to share it, I will print it and put it in the hands of every inmate I see."

David did share it. I printed his testimony and took hundreds of copies with me to the prisons. It did not take long for it to get to the media. Wow! You talk about bloodhounds. They can find you. I think I talked to every major network and told them that David was now a son of God and did not want to discuss his past. They persisted.

Once I was in a motel in Newburgh, New York, and I was going to visit David. Mary Murphy, an award-winning newscaster in New York City, called my room and invited me to eat in the dining room, as she wanted to be the first to interview David. She was a very nice lady, but I told her no.

I went back to my room, and then there was a knock on the door. Investigative journalist Maury Terry and Wayne Darwen, a producer from *Inside Edition*, were at the door. I also told them no about an interview, but they politely kept asking if they could come in. I let them in, and they said, "Look, we don't care what he talks about. He can talk about Jesus for two hours, and you can be in the room to stop the interview at any time."

I said, "I'm gonna see him tomorrow. I'll ask him. If he says no, then it will be no!"

I saw David in the prison visiting room the next day. To my surprise, he said, "Brother Don, I believe the time is right for me to tell what Jesus has done for me."

David Berkowitz is my friend. He shared his testimony with me after our meeting in 1988. This is the account of God's more-than-amazing grace reaching into the depraved, dark world of David Berkowitz, freeing him from his torment, and giving him forgiveness, eternal life, and sonship in the family of God. Here are a couple of his favorite scriptures:

> I will praise You, O LORD, with my whole heart; I will tell of all Your marvelous works. I will be glad and rejoice in You; I will sing praise to Your name, O Most High.
> —PSALM 9:1–2

> If the Son sets you free, you will be free indeed.
> —JOHN 8:36, ESV

David says that as a child he was vicious and destructive. I recall him telling me how he craved the darkness. He said, "Like the psalmist says, I must truly thank my wonderful God for His abundant love, grace, and mercy. You see, since my childhood, I have been tormented and victimized by demons. During all of my childhood and for much of my adult life, cruel demons had control of me. But thanks be to Jesus Christ, I was able to be restored to my right mind."

David's story has been chronicled by newspapers and other

media outlets since the crimes took place in the mid-seventies. However, the complete truth has yet to be written because the complete truth is that David did not act alone in the Son of Sam crimes. He has told me often about his tormented childhood.

There was a time in my life when I was living in complete rebellion against God. I was so wicked that I was actually worshipping the devil, and I was involved with satanism. Looking back at all that has happened to me, it is no surprise that I fell into such depravity. I was demon possessed.

Let me tell you what some of my life was like when I was just a small child. When I was little, I would often have fits in which I would roll on the floor and knock over furniture. My adopted mother, who has long since passed away, would have no control over me. I was so vicious and destructive that I often caused considerable property damage.

When I was in public school, I was so violent and disruptive that a teacher once grabbed me in a headlock and threw me out of his classroom. I was so much trouble that my parents were ordered by the school officials to take me to a child psychologist every week. But this had no effect.

David told me that he would get so depressed that he used to hide under his bed for hours. Then at other times he would lock himself in a closet and sit in total darkness from morning until afternoon. He said, "I craved the darkness and felt an urge to flee away from people."

DRIVEN INTO THE DARKENED STREETS

Other times I would wake up in the middle of the night, sneak out of the house, and wander the streets. I recall a force that would drive me into the darkened streets, even in inclement weather, where I roamed the streets like an alley cat in the darkness.

Sometimes at 3:00 or 4:00 in the morning I would sneak back into the house the same way I left, by climbing the fire escape. My parents would not even know that I was gone.

I continually worried and frightened my parents because I behaved so strangely. At times I would go an entire day without talking to them. I'd walk around our apartment, talking to myself. My parents knew that I lived in an imaginary world, but they could do nothing about it. From time to time I would see my parents break down and cry because they saw that I was such a tormented person.

David said growing up was a nightmare and that thoughts of suicide plagued him continually. "I was so depressed and haunted that I would also spend time sitting on the window ledge of my bedroom with my legs dangling over the side. My parents would yell at me to get in, but I seldom listened to them. I would feel such an urge to push myself out the window that my body would tremble violently. And we lived on the sixth floor!"

POSSESSED

His adopted parents did the best they could, but David was not able to respond to their love and direction.

My mom and dad tried to bring me up as best as they could. They loved me and gave me everything that good parents would give to their only child. But I was so wild, mixed-up, and crazy that I could barely hang on to my sanity. Even when I would walk down the streets, there always seemed to be a force that would try to make me step in front of moving cars.

I was overwhelmed with thoughts about dying. And I wasn't even a teenager! I had no idea what to do, and neither did my parents. They tried to raise me in the Jewish faith, but they knew nothing about Jesus, the Messiah of Israel.

Many of the things that happened to me might shock some people. But none of this was a shock to the Lord. In His day, when our Savior walked among humanity, cases of children being victimized and possessed by evil spirits were very common. [See Mark 7:24–30 and 9:17–29.]

In fact, childhood possession cases still happen today. But modern psychology tends to dismiss these disturbed children and blame their problems on some type of organic brain damage, or family problems, or something within the child's environment, etc.

There were a few times in my life when I was at a stage of equilibrium. I managed to finish high school even though most of the time I was truant or in trouble. I also spent three years in the army. I was honorably discharged in 1974. But even in the service I had problems.

PULLED INTO THE OCCULT

David returned from his service in the armed forces to a lonely environment. The few friends he had before he was in the army had moved away. His adopted mother had died. His father had remarried and also moved away. Then he was invited to a party where he met some new friends. He didn't know they were satanists, and it didn't really matter when he found out that they were.

In 1975 I had become heavily involved with the occult and witchcraft. Looking back, I cannot even begin to explain how I had gotten involved. It seemed that one day everything magically fell into place. Books about witchcraft seemed to pop up all around me. Everywhere I looked, there appeared a sign or symbol pointing me to Satan. It felt as if a mighty power was reaching out to me.

I had no peace of mind. I felt as if I was being pulled along by a powerful force. I had no idea how to fight it, and to be honest, I didn't try to. Why? Because things just seemed to be falling into place in a supernatural way.

To someone who has never been involved in the occult, this could be hard to understand. But for people who have been involved, they know full well what I am referring to. The power leading me could not be resisted, at least not without Jesus. But I had no relationship with the Lord Jesus at this time, and so I had no defense against the devil.

In the Bible, Jesus said about Satan: "He was a murderer from the beginning, not holding to the truth, for there is no truth in him. When he lies, he speaks his native language, for he is a liar and the father of lies" [John 8:44, NIV].

Well, he certainly lied to me! For during the years 1976 and 1977 I had been lied to and deceived. And as a result of listening to him, I wound up in prison with a sentence of three hundred and fifty consecutive years. I was charged with six murders and a number of other shootings and crimes.

I have seen enough of the demonic things his satanic cult was involved in. I have been to many of the crime scenes and places where the group met. The group often met at Untermyer Park in Yonkers, New York. They built satanic altars and sacrificed German shepherd dogs. I have been there and stood in defiance on the very altar. Friends who were with me got sick, and one broke out in hives as they left the area. The altar is no longer there. I have been in the vacant caretaker's house. SOS was spray-painted all over. They used the one-room house to party and plan. There is a hospital across from the area, and reports circulated of hospital employees hearing horrible screams coming from there in the night.

Don Dickerman standing in defiance at the site where Berkowitz's group built satanic altars and sacrificed German shepherds

The Son of Sam crimes were an ugly chapter in American history. As the late Dr. E. V. Hill, a Los Angeles pastor, used to say, "Thank God for Jesus!"

LIFE IN PRISON

David has a large scar on the left side of his throat from an attempt on his life while at Attica.

> As with many inmates, life in prison has been a big struggle. I have had my share of problems and hassles. At one time I almost lost my life when another inmate

cut my throat. Yet through all this, God had His loving hands on me.

Over the years I have met a number of men who had accepted Christ. Many of them tried to witness to me. But because of the extent to which the devil had me bound, it was very hard for me to truly understand the gospel. However, about 1987, I did accept Jesus as my Lord and Savior. And today I cannot thank Him enough for all He has done for me.

Presently the Lord is using me to teach Bible studies in the chapel, as well as to give words of encouragement during our services. In addition, I have the authorization to work with the men whom the Department of Correctional Services has labeled "mentally disturbed" or who are slow learners. I have been able to counsel these troubled people and help them with some of their spiritual and physical needs.

One of my favorite passages of Scripture is found in the Old Testament Book of Micah the prophet. This passage has become to me something of my love song to the Lord.

> Who is a God like you, who pardons sin and forgives the transgression of the remnant of his inheritance? You do not stay angry forever but delight to show mercy. You will again have compassion on us; you will tread our sins underfoot and hurl all our iniquities into the depths of the sea. You will be faithful to Jacob, and show love to Abraham, as you pledged on oath to our ancestors in days long ago.
> —MICAH 7:18–20, NIV

When David and I first met face-to-face, I could tell by looking into his eyes that he was saved, and he confirmed it when I asked him. From that night, for whatever reason, David and I have become very good friends. He has given me much insight into the demonic realm. He has been on both sides. David calls me his pastor today.

Demon possession is very real, but it cannot happen to a believer. David's testimony is that the more he filled himself with the Word of God, the freer he became, and today he is demon free. The tormentors now can only influence his life and thinking. He can be oppressed, but when he was lost, he was possessed.

David's message today is summed up in one of his favorite scriptures: "To him who loves us and has freed us from our sins by his blood, and has made us to be a kingdom and priests to serve his God and Father—to him be glory and power for ever and ever! Amen" (Rev. 1:5–6, NIV).

David has many friends who write to him and help support him. Some have helped to develop a website. To learn more about David Berkowitz and to read some of his personal writings, please visit his website at ariseandshine.org.

HERE YA GO
preacher

DON DICKERMAN
BOX 575
HURST, TEXAS 76053

NORTH BAY, CA
PM
23 JUN
1988

USA

Chapter 6

THE WIDOW:
BETTY LOU BEETS

DEATH ROW REDEMPTION

ETTY LOU BEETS was born in North Carolina. There is limited information available about her childhood. Betty contracted measles as a young child and was deaf as a result. She claimed that she was sexually abused from the age of five by her father and other men acquainted with him. It appears that Betty's mother had to be institutionalized when Betty was twelve, leaving Betty with the responsibility of caring for her two younger siblings.

When she was only fifteen years old, Betty married Robert Franklin Branson. After her conviction for murder, Betty claimed that all her marriages had been abusive, but that didn't stop her from attempting suicide when she and Branson separated at one point. They did get back together after the suicide attempt, and they tried to make their marriage work. However, they eventually divorced in 1969. This was five years before I preached in my first prison. Little did I know that I would someday minister to the infamous black widow.

A year later, in 1970, Betty married Bill York Lane. It seemed that Betty just experienced more of the same—misery and abuse. During one incident, Bill broke her nose. Her response was to shoot him twice in the back. Betty was charged with attempted murder, but the charges were dropped when her husband confessed that he threatened Betty's life before she shot him. Betty and Bill divorced after the shooting, but after the charges were dropped, they remarried, only to divorce again shortly thereafter. I wonder what it was that kept Betty going back to abusive men.

Betty's third husband was Ronnie C. Threlkold. They married in 1978, but the marriage ended when Betty tried to run over Ronnie with her vehicle. She married again in 1979. The remains of her fourth husband, Doyle Wayne Barker, were

The Widow: Betty Lou Beets

found buried in the backyard of Betty's house, underneath a shed. He had been shot in the head. More disturbing is that Betty had revealed her plans to her daughter Shirley ahead of time, and Shirley helped her bury the body.

In 1982, Betty married her fifth husband, Jimmy Don Beets. It was the investigation into Jimmy's disappearance that eventually led to Betty's arrest, trial, conviction, and execution.

Once again, Betty involved one of her adult children in her crime. On August 6, 1983, Betty told her son Robert to leave the house because she was going to kill her husband. Her son left, and when he returned, Jimmy Don Beets was dead, with two bullets in his head. Betty and Robert buried Jimmy's body in a wishing well in the front yard. Betty then phoned the police and falsely reported that Jimmy was missing.

Two years later the police had gathered enough evidence to arrest Betty for murder. The bodies of her two victims were found during a search of her property. Shirley and Robert were charged in connection with the crimes as well. They both testified against their mother at her trial. Betty pleaded not guilty, and when she testified, she claimed that her children had pulled the trigger, not her. The jury didn't believe her, and she was found guilty of the capital murder of Jimmy Don Beets on October 11, 1985.

Over more than ten years there were several appeals, one of which resulted in a rehearing of the case, but the conviction and sentence remained the same. Although evidence about the murder of Barker was presented at her trial, she was never tried for the murder of her fourth husband since she was sentenced to death for the murder of her fifth husband.[1]

I had heard of Betty Lou Beets before I actually met her. As a minister who went regularly to minister to the ladies on

Texas's death row, I knew her from a distance. I found it interesting that her crimes took place in Gun Barrel City since her conviction was for murdering her husband with a gun.

Betty was always present at our Bible studies on death row, but she was always silent. When I saw Betty Lou Beets, I thought she looked like a typical grandmother. I am not sure how she communicated since she was deaf, but there was never an interpreter with her when I was there. She always had a big, welcoming smile though. Even with all the times I was on death row, I never really got to know her, probably because of the communication challenges related to her deafness.

In that death row area, the dayroom, or meeting place, was surrounded by the cells, and there was a small wall that had an entryway to get into the meeting area, where there were chairs. Betty stayed on the outer perimeter of the dayroom area, against the wall. She observed, but she never engaged in the conversation. She was, however, always there. I am not sure if she was able to read lips, so I don't know if she ever understood what was being said during the Bible studies.

Betty Lou Beets was executed by lethal injection on February 24, 2000, in Texas's Huntsville Unit. Did Betty repent? Did she accept Christ? I can only say that I certainly hope so.

AERE YA GO
preacher

DON DICKERMAN
BOX 575
HURST, TEXAS 76053

NORTH BAY, CA 949
PM
I A
23 JUN
1988

USA

Chapter 7

WOMEN ON DEATH ROW: FRANCES NEWTON, PAM PERILLO, AND KARLA FAYE TUCKER

DEATH ROW REDEMPTION

As we saw in the last chapter, not all the people who end up on death row are men. During my time ministering in prisons, I befriended several women on death row, including Frances Newton, Pam Perillo, and Karla Faye Tucker.

EVIDENCE?

I met Frances Newton on death row, and we became friends. I never knew her without a pretty, peaceful smile. She was always at the Bible studies.

Frances was the third woman executed in Texas since capital punishment was reinstated in 1982. She was also the first Black woman executed in Texas since the Civil War. What's more, she may have been innocent. There was an article in the *Austin Chronicle* titled "Without Evidence: Executing Frances Newton—Another Texas Death Row Case Marked by Official Carelessness, Negligence, and Intransigence." The article stated, "For there is no incontrovertible evidence against Newton, and the paltry evidence that does exist has been completely compromised."[1]

The article recounts the Harris County prosecutors' version of the story:

> Newton is a coldblooded killer who murdered her husband and two young children inside the family's apartment outside Houston on April 7, 1987, by shooting each of them, executionstyle, in order to collect life insurance. Newton had the opportunity, they argued during her 1988 trial, and a motive—a troubled relationship with her husband, Adrian, and the promise of $100,000 in insurance money from policies she'd recently taken out on his life and on the life of their 21-month-old daughter Farrah. And she had the means, they say: a .25caliber Raven Arms pistol she had allegedly stolen from a boyfriend's house.[2]

The article also makes a pretty compelling argument about the possible execution of an innocent woman. Frances maintained her innocence to the end. She also suggested a plausible theory for the killings. Her husband was a drug addict and owed $1,500 to a drug dealer, and Frances believes the drug dealer shot her husband and kids.

The initial investigation revealed evidence—or rather lack of evidence—that pointed to Frances' innocence. For example, since a bullet lodged in her husband's head, the shooter would have had blood and brain matter on them, confirmed by a trail of blood in the hallway. And, of course, the shooter would have had gunshot residue on their hands and clothing. Investigators found no gunshot residue on Newton's hands or on the sleeves of the sweater she wore that day. There were also no traces of blood on any of her clothing.[3]

Personally, I want to believe she was innocent. I do know Frances was saved, and she did not fear death. She spent almost seventeen years on death row and was executed by lethal injection on September 14, 2005.

IMPRISONMENT TO REDEMPTION

Pam Perillo was another one of my buddies on Texas's death row.

In 1980, Pam, along with married couple Mike Briddle and Linda Fletcher, robbed and murdered Robert Banks and Bob Skeens. Pam and her friends were hitchhiking in Houston when Banks picked them up and offered to pay them to help him move. Banks even treated them to a meal at a local restaurant, but at that meal Pam and her friends observed that Banks had quite a bit of cash in his wallet. That set in motion the tragic events that followed.

Banks let the three friends spend the night and invited them to a rodeo the next day. When they returned back to Banks' home, his friend Bob Skeens was there to help with the move. When Banks and Skeens went to buy coffee and donuts for everyone the next morning, Pam and Briddle armed themselves with two of Banks' guns. When the two men returned, they were tied up at gunpoint and robbed. Pam found a cassette recorder that they used to record mocking recreations of murders. The three friends then strangled both men with rope around their necks. Fletcher testified that Pam said, "I don't like looking at you; your face is turning blue," while Skeens was being strangled.

The three friends were all eventually arrested. Fletcher received five years' probation for aggravated robbery. Briddle was convicted of capital murder, sentenced to death, and executed in 1995. Pam was tried twice because of an error during her first trial. Both times she was convicted of capital murder and sentenced to death.

In 1996, Pam filed a petition for habeas corpus, and the court determined her trial attorney had a conflict of interest. She received a stay of execution two days before her scheduled execution. The federal district court vacated the judgment against her and gave the State of Texas the choice to either retry her or release her. The end result was that Pam made a deal to lessen her sentence from death by lethal injection to a life sentence.[4]

Pam gave her life to the Lord when she was in the county jail, before she was sent to death row. Her embrace of the Christian faith led to her sharing the gospel with her fellow inmates so they could experience freedom and redemption too. It has been said, "Although Pamela's story is one of imprisonment—first by abuse and addiction and ultimately behind the locked doors of the criminal justice system—it's also a story of hope—of finding a new path in faith, and of taking courage from the promise of salvation."[5]

I remember sitting beside Pam during one of our Bible studies. After some singing, I asked her if she thought I was a good singer. She smiled politely and said, "Can I take the fifth amendment on that?" Then her smile got bigger. "Let me just say I have heard better, but you are pretty good."

THE PERSONIFICATION OF EVIL

At age eight, Karla Faye Tucker was smoking marijuana. By the age of ten she was shooting heroin, and when she was fourteen, she had already turned a few tricks in Houston. At age twenty, after an unsuccessful marriage, she became an active prostitute. By the time her crimes took place at age twenty-three, she was doing drugs virtually nonstop, taking all kinds of pills and shooting amphetamines into her veins. Many times she has told me that she liked the idea of being "big, bad, and mean."

That was certainly the reputation she carried with her to the courtroom. The chilling events on the early morning of June 13, 1983, stand alone in the annals of Texas crime history. That was the night Karla Faye Tucker and her boyfriend, Daniel Garrett, snuck into a Houston apartment and committed two brutal murders. Using a pickax, they hacked a man and woman to death and left the ax embedded in the woman's chest. The jury found her guilty of capital murder and sentenced her to death.

From left: Karla Faye Tucker, Pam Perillo, and Frances Newton

I don't think anyone except Karla's family was disappointed when she was sentenced to die by lethal injection in the Texas death chamber. Karla told me, "My family has stuck by me over the years and shown me the love and support I have needed."

When Karla took the stand during her trial, she told of killing Jerry Dean, a man she genuinely hated, and Deborah Ruth Thornton, a woman she did not know. Thornton apparently was just spending the night with Dean. Her testimony included the account of Garrett beating the man with a hammer and how she took the pickax and hit him to stop the gurgling sound that was coming from his body. She told of the woman begging for her assailants to mercifully kill her while she had a pickax embedded in her shoulder. The self-portrait Karla painted in the Houston courtroom in 1983 was one of a twisted, pathetic, drugged-out woman who showed no mercy on a pleading, innocent victim.

Charley Davidson, a former prosecutor, gave this impression of the demonic countenance he saw as Karla came into the courtroom. "I just remember that when she came into court... her attitude and the way she looked and everything about her was the personification of evil. When she was in court...you didn't even want to turn your back."[6]

Karla Faye Tucker was a bitter, angry, confused, twisted

young woman when she made the poorest decision of her life. A broken self-esteem and a desire to be accepted, coupled with anger and bitterness, made her vulnerable to foolish acts. She was ruled by a hatred she could not control. That combined with drugs that numbed her conscience and intensified her negative emotions made for a deadly mixture.

As is the case with so many on death row, Karla's childhood was tragic. Her mother and father divorced. We can never know the full impact family disintegration has on a child. The feuding and anger that generally precede divorce leave scars much deeper than we can know. She and her two sisters lived with her father for a while. Karla said it was hard for her father to take care of little girls, and after a short period of time they moved in with her mother.

Karla's mother was an alcoholic and drug abuser. When those things get a grip on your life, you can never be the person you want to be or hope to be. Karla's mother did secretarial work by day and prostitution by night. Karla was not aware of her mother's nighttime activities until she was fourteen years old. Karla loved her family very much and did not blame her problems on them.

"I know that when I first smoked pot, it's because I saw my sisters smoking it, and I told them I was going to tell on them, so they made me smoke it so I wouldn't tell on them," Karla said. "You can't blame something like that [crime] on anybody else but yourself. I alone am responsible for what I have done. I had my choices."

Karla's life was out of order at a young age. She repeated the seventh grade three times and hated school. When she finally made it to the eighth grade, she decided to quit. I asked her about any good memories she might have from school, and she said she had none. There was no one in Karla's life to encourage her; she had no reason to want to excel or compete. That is the sad story of much of American youth today.

Homicide detective J. C. Mosier said, "I don't want to see her die. I believe in the death penalty, and she's not the only person I've ever sent to Death Row. But in most cases, they're bad people, period. She never had a chance from the start. There was no way for her to go but bad."[7]

This is not an acceptable excuse. Other kids grow up in similar conditions, and they don't commit heinous crimes. Some even become successful people. However, if you took a survey of almost two million Americans locked up today,[8] you would find the vast majority come from dysfunctional homes. Drug-related crimes account for over 20 percent of the crimes committed today.[9]

Karla believed that if she had not been using drugs, she would not have been involved in the killings. But she said, "If the killings had not occurred, I would still be on drugs. I wanted to [do drugs], and I continued to do it I guess because I liked it. I liked the feeling. What can I say? Everyone was doing it. I guess that's got to do with people wanting to fit in."

People go where they are accepted, and the drug community will accept anyone. It means money for the pushers and company for the misery—and misery loves company!

NOT THE SAME PERSON

The first time I heard of Karla Faye Tucker, I was walking from the chapel at the Riverside Unit with Chaplain Kathleen O'Brien. The chaplain, a good friend, asked if I had met the new girl on death row, an ax murderer named Karla Faye Tucker.

Karla was at Mountain View Unit in Gatesville, Texas. The

first time I met with the death row people there, we were in the administrative segregation section of the prison. Only two women were on death row at that time: Pamela Perillo and Karla Faye Tucker.

The conditions were not very conducive to worship. The area was small and depressing, and the noise from boisterous, angry inmates in punitive cells was extremely distracting. The death row ladies were eventually moved to a separate building on the prison grounds. It was actually somewhat peaceful. The cells were painted white, and the women added personal touches to the cells. The concrete floors, the cold steel cells, and the red brick walls reminded you that you were in prison, but the atmosphere created by the ladies was livable.

There was a small exercise yard, a grassy area similar to a small front yard. It was well kept and—except for the tall cyclone fence surrounding it—attractive, with a flower bed and neatly edged grass. Usually the death row cat could be seen in this area. The women also took care of the cat.

My first impression of Karla, a young woman with such a brutal reputation, was one of disbelief. She seemed so peaceful and content, even with an attitude of excitement. How could this be the cold, uncaring ax murderer I had heard so much about? Others had told me she claimed to be a Christian now, with a measure of doubt in their voices, as if to say, "Don't all of those death row people get religion?"

Let me address that thought a little bit. I have been on death row in many states, and I have conducted worship services on death row. Recently, I was at the death row housing unit in Florence, Arizona. There are 102 men on death row there. This was a special worship service, publicized and talked about by the inmates themselves because an out-of-state evangelist would be there. Four men came to the service. To say "Don't they all get religion?" is a calloused and false assumption.

While being under the sentence of death certainly would make one seriously examine their life and consider the claims of Jesus Christ, not everyone on death row "gets religion." Death at the hands of the state is a heavy cloud to wake up under each day.

Death row inmates are approached by many Christians through the mail, telling them of God's great love and forgiveness. Loving chaplains are available to minister to them and answer their questions about God. Perhaps for the first time in their lives, these people come in contact with the truth of the gospel. Perhaps they have never been told they are loved unconditionally and that God's forgiveness includes even the worst of sinners. Yet if you go to death row and have a worship service, only a handful of those allowed to leave their cells will attend.

I believe Karla Faye Tucker was saved, genuinely born again. I believe those who knew her best share these same feelings. Chaplain Tim Crosby smiles when he talks about her. You might expect to hear this testimony from her chaplain and from me, a prison evangelist and personal friend. That is also the account given by officers who were around her virtually all the time and are familiar with inmates and convict games; they will tell you that Karla was a "gem."

Not only did prison officials verify her genuineness, but relatives of her victims forgave her and worked on her behalf to try to get her off death row. Prosecutors, arresting officers, and defense attorneys all spoke of the great change in her life. *Rehabilitation* was not the proper word for her. Something greater than a positive adjustment in her life took place. Anyone who knew Karla Faye Tucker in the early 1980s and then knew her after she was born again would tell you that something miraculous happened. She was not the same person.

Many years ago, attorney Henry Oncken was asked to describe his relationship with Karla. He had been appointed by a judge to defend her. "I couldn't stand her when I first met her. She was just dragged out on drugs and just had that I don't care attitude. Slovenly, slurred speech, and sleepy-eyed."

As the drugs worked their way out of Karla's system while she was in the county jail, Oncken began to see her in a different light. "She is someone I've developed a liking for, a fondness for," said Oncken. He took his wife and daughter to visit Karla one Christmas. She had a gift for him, a sweater she had knitted just for him. "The person who is Karla Faye Tucker today is not the same person who was Karla Faye Tucker at that time."[10]

He further said, "I never lose sight of the fact that she killed two people with a pickax. The person who did that I have a terrible dislike for, but this is not the same person." Oncken said also that he truly believes she changed. "I know what she was. I know she has changed. She is a person who has a tremendous capacity to love someone. It is very unusual; I could go for a long time and maybe never find someone in a similar circumstance that would make me say such things."[11]

Even though many people worked to save her, Karla Faye Tucker was executed by lethal injection on February 3, 1998.

I would like to share a letter from Karla, written to me several years before her death.

Dear Don:

I do hope this letter finds you in good spirits (and not upset with me). I'm really sorry it has taken me until now to write back. I'm so lazy when it comes to writing. Please pray for me that I will quit procrastinating when it comes to my letter writing.

I just want you to know how very much I enjoyed your visit! I know I must have you wondering about that because of how long it has taken me to write, but I really did enjoy the visit!

Since you've been here, I've had the chance to read a book called *In His Steps* by Charles M. Sheldon and it is a wonderful book. If you haven't had the chance to read it, then if you ever get the time, you would really enjoy it. It is great, so motivational!

Don, I have also signed up for my second semester of college. I am taking English literature 2302 and history 2301. I am really loving going to school and making use of my brain instead of just clouding it with drugs! I also got my GED graduation class ring. It is beautiful; the stone in it is black onyx and it has the year on it. I am so proud of it I could bust!

Well, Don, I reckon I'll close here, I just wanted to say hi and to tell you, you are in all of my prayers. I did enjoy the visit and the Bible study was great. We are blessed to have people like yourself that care enough about people to help them and believe in them. Thanks to God, and thank you, Don. May God bless you!

LOVE, KARLA

This was a pretty typical letter from Karla—down-to-earth with a little bit of excitement about picking up some of life that she missed along the way. I never saw Karla down; she was always smiling and had positive things to say.

WE HAVE PEACE

Karla and her good friend Pam Perillo told me of a visit with journalists from England who did an interview and then wanted some pictures. The photographer said, "Don't smile. You're on death row; you're supposed to look sad." The ladies refused to look sad. They both said, "We are not sad. We are saved, and we have peace."

I'd like to say a word about Pam. She spent twenty years on death row. I did a video interview with Karla and Pam many years ago. Two of my ministry associates, Charlie Paris and Tom Goodson, were there to run the cameras. I reviewed that video a few days ago, and tears came to my eyes as I heard Pam tell of how she came to know Jesus Christ.

She said, "I thought when they sent you to death row that they killed you then. I didn't know nothing about automatic appeals and such. So I really began to search for God. I was so scared. I prayed, and He came. He really came into my life and changed me that moment. I have not feared death since then. That was at the Goree Unit in Huntsville, before they moved us over here to Mountain View. In 1980, that's when I was saved."

Pam told me she spent most of her young life in juvenile halls and foster homes. She never made it to junior high school. Pam said, "I guess my home life was fairly normal until my mother died at age ten. That's when everything sort of started falling apart. My father started drinking, and it just went downhill from there." At about age thirteen Pam had been using drugs long enough to reach out for heavier, stronger drugs and was shooting heroin in her first year as a teenager. "Things just got progressively worse."

Both Pam and Karla testify that if drugs had not been a

part of their lives, they would not be on death row. Both were heroin users. Very few get out from under the curse of King Heroin, as they call it on the streets. It made slaves out of these two women.

I asked Pam if there was a point in her life of drug abuse when she could sense she would never get out of heroin's grip?

> No, not really. The drugs just more or less blind you to reality. Sure, you try [to quit]. You kick and get strung out, kick and get strung out. But no, you can't quit, and there was a point where I would listen to no one. I always knew what I was doing was wrong and that I was getting worse, but at that time I didn't care. I just didn't care. I liked what I was doing!

I asked Pam what her greatest desire was. I was surprised when she didn't say, "To get out of here." Instead she said, "To see my little boy grow up—that's what I want most of all." Her son was a year old when she was sentenced to die in 1980.

Pam has a quiet and likable personality. Karla's personality was bubbly yet genuine. She liked to joke and cut up. Both ladies were a delight to be around, and I grew to love them very much. It was a sad day in my life when Karla was executed.

I asked Karla if she had any advice to young people who might be using drugs. "Yes, I would first start off by trying to tell them what I've been through, what all I went through in my experience, and how I found Jesus. I would emphasize what a difference He makes. He really made a difference in me."

Both Pam and Karla agreed that most likely their words of warning will go unheeded. They know that others tried to warn them of the dangers. Seldom do we learn from listening. What a sad comment on humanity. We are able, somehow, to believe it will never happen to us. We tell ourselves that we are the exception. Most inmates will tell you the same thing. "I never thought I would get caught. I never thought I would become addicted. You couldn't make me believe that I would be an alcoholic." What a powerful deception of the enemy in the world today.

When inmates deal with the trauma of their human failure, the guilt and shame are intense. They basically fall into two categories. Some come to a realization that something is wrong in their life and begin to seek help from God. Then there are others who recognize their problem but feel it is wrong to turn to God only after they are in trouble. Perhaps a third category are those who accept their place in life as "that's just the way I am" and go about their business. Those people seldom change.

As Karla's system was purged of the drugs when she was in jail, she began to think more clearly. She knew something was wrong in her life, but she was still dealing with her desire to be big, bad, and mean. She told me:

> A group from Teen Challenge came to the Harris County Jail with a puppet show. Many people had been asking me to go to church and to go to the Bible studies, but I was not interested.
>
> Actually, the only reason I went to church this time was because everyone in my tank went, and there was no one left to talk to. So I went more or less just so I could visit with others. The most amazing thing [happened]. I heard about Jesus and forgiveness, and I felt such a warm, loving feeling that drew me to Him. I knew I had done something so terrible that I didn't even think God could forgive me. I didn't think He could even love me. That day I received Jesus in a real simple sort of way, but He made such a difference in my life, I can't even explain.
>
> If people who get into drugs only knew what Jesus

could do, they would never desire anything else. I doubt if anyone could have told me that though. There was a point in my life when I didn't listen to nobody. No one could tell me anything. It is so sad that I had to have such a terrible experience before I found Him.

He makes a difference in what you feel and how you feel about things. You can always overcome anything when you have Jesus to help you. I know that now. I know that. I wish I could divide myself in a million pieces and go tell the whole world about Him. In a sense I now have that opportunity because of all the news media and exposure that is intended to be negative.

What Satan means for evil, God uses for good. God is able to turn the most destructive situations into something of beauty. He is faithful to do that.

Pam and Karla were not only at peace with God, but they possessed the peace of God. Pam said, "We are not sad. We have kind officers who treat us right. We all get along with each other, and we work at not being in a gloomy and sad situation. We are not depressed." That is one of the beauties of knowing Christ Jesus in a personal, intimate way—He really does give peace and contentment in otherwise depressing situations. He is Lord of everything and every circumstance.

As we continued our discussion, we each shared some favorite Bible passages. Pam said, "One of my favorite chapters in the Bible is Romans chapter 8, where it says nothing can separate me from the love of God which is in Christ Jesus. That includes all of the feelings you experience on death row. I read that or quote that to myself just about every night. What goes after this life is going to be better, and I believe that. I hold on to that belief. This same chapter tells me that if God be for me, who can be against me?"

Karla said,

> You know, there's another difference that God can make in somebody's life. I've noticed it in mine. When you've grown up around people and you're acting bad all your life, you believe you have to have this wall in front of you and you don't care about this or anything. Then when Jesus comes into your life, that wall just comes tumbling right down to the ground. And I can get along with anybody now, whereas before, I don't even think I really tried. I can get along with anyone, and it's not like all that pressure is hitting me to be bad and fit in. And trouble doesn't even follow me anymore. He's protecting me!

I have been ministering in prisons since 1974. I can say without much second thought that I have met only a handful of people like Karla Faye Tucker. I have personally talked to thousands of inmates. I have met all kinds, from all backgrounds, all races, the full gamut of crimes, and I doubt I will meet one that surprises me with what he or she may have done. Karla Faye Tucker stood out!

Her salvation was genuine. Her countenance reflected a deep inner peace, her personality radiated with joy, and her soul possessed much compassion. She had Christlike qualities that cannot be learned; they must be received. She was caring and tender. She studied her Bible and knew it well.

Karla wrote:

> From time to time over the years it gets really, really rough, but Jesus never said it would be easy. In fact, He said there would be tribulation, but not to worry because He had overcome the world. In the hard times Jesus promised to give me strength and peace, and He has never failed me! There are those who will always doubt my change, but

DEATH ROW REDEMPTION

that's OK too. The only thing that really matters now is that Jesus knows, and I know that I devoted my life to serving Him and saving lives for Him now....After emotionally alienating my family for so many years due to my drug abuse, Jesus helped me tear down my walls, and now my family and I are closer than we have ever been! My whole attitude towards life has changed. I am a new person in Jesus, and although the road has been hard, here I sit, at peace on death row. But believe me it would not be possible without Jesus Christ in my life![12]

Don Dickerman
Box 575
Hurst, Texas 76053

Here ya go preacher

Chapter 8

THE MEANEST MAN IN SOUTH CAROLINA: DONALD "PEE WEE" GASKINS

D ONALD "PEE WEE" Gaskins, called the meanest man in South Carolina, was a serial killer considered to be one of the state's most notorious criminals. He was sent to reform school when he was thirteen for hitting a young woman in the head with an ax while breaking into her home. He had a long criminal history, including assault, burglary, sexual assault, manslaughter, and murder.

Gaskins was arrested in 1975 for the final time when one of his criminal associates told police Gaskins had murdered half brothers Dennis Bellamy and Johnny Knight. When police searched land near Gaskins's home, they found the bodies of eight of his victims. While Gaskins eventually confessed to killing over one hundred people, he was confirmed to have killed only fifteen people, including a toddler.

Gaskins was tried and convicted of murder in 1976. He was initially sentenced to death, but that sentence was commuted to life in prison. However, in 1982 he used explosives to murder Rudolph Tyner, a death row inmate he was hired to kill. For that crime, Gaskins was again sentenced to death.

So how did I know Pee Wee? I had preached at the old South Carolina Penitentiary, where death row was located until 1990, so I probably met him there, although I don't recall it. Death row is now located at the Broad River Correctional Institution in Columbia, South Carolina, and I went there to preach. There were two levels of cellblocks, with a large dayroom in the center where the service was held. A good-sized group came to the service, and while many of the inmates stayed in their cells, they could hear the service.

After the service, Chaplain Brown said, "There is a man up on the second tier that wants to see you." As we walked toward the stairs, he said, "It's Pee Wee Gaskins." I didn't know who

The Meanest Man in South Carolina: Donald "Pee Wee" Gaskins

he was, as his name was not known in Texas. Chaplain Brown was surprised and told me he would be executed soon. When we got to his cell, I could see why he was called Pee Wee—he was only about five feet four inches tall. He had a haggard look about him, but he did not look dangerous.

He said, "I heard all of the worship service, and I agree with everything you said. Thank you for caring for people like me. I am ready to go, and I'm not nervous about it." He said he would like to correspond with me, and we exchanged addresses. A few days later I received a letter from Pee Wee. I wrote him back, but he was executed before he could respond.

Dear Rev. Dickerman,

It was sure great to see you this last Wednesday and thank you for coming up to see me. I really enjoyed meeting you and Chaplain Brown. I do get to see Chaplain Brown almost every week and we talk as much as we can.

I'm writing this letter as I promised you I would and to let you know that this week, I think it will be Thursday night September 6th right after midnight. As I told you I'll be more ready than most if it must be this way. In fact if it was tonight I'd not worry about where I would go.

As I told you and Chaplain Brown, my religion is something I want to keep between myself and God and nothing to the press as they like to run things in the ground and I'd be one they would have a field day with if they knew one way or the other how my life ends.

I have very [few of] my friends that I'll be writing from now on and this may be my last letter to you on the account that I don't know from one day to the next where I'll be or if I still have this typewriter. I won't be able to write anyone without it because my hands are in very bad shape from arthritis, so God bless you my friend and all of your friends. I hope any enemy you have will turn their lives over to Christ.

God bless you my friend,

A brother in Christ,

Donald H. "Pee Wee" Gaskins Jr.

I never heard from Pee Wee again. He was executed by electric chair on September 6, 1991.

Here Ya Go
preacher

Don Dickerman
Box 575
Hurst, Texas 76053

Chapter 9

SERIAL KILLER: TED BUNDY

I T WAS IN the visiting area for death row inmates and attorneys and ministers at Florida State Prison that I first met Ted Bundy while I visited another inmate. Bundy was visiting with his attorney, and I was visiting with then death row inmate George Lemon. I did not recognize Bundy, although I knew about him and his crimes, but he recognized me.

Bundy was seated across the partition and to my left. He stood up and said, "Excuse me, are you Don Dickerman?" I said yes, and although he was handcuffed, he extended his hands forward to shake my hand. "Hey, I'm Ted Bundy. I see you when you preach in our chapel [an inmate had developed a system to televise chapel services back to death row], and your newsletter that you send is read by everyone on the row." We talked for a minute, and he asked if he could write to me.

THE KILLER

Although most people know his name, some readers may not know about Bundy and how he came to be known as one of the most notorious killers of all time. His story begins in childhood, like virtually all inmates. Born out of wedlock, Bundy initially thought his mother was his sister and his grandparents were his parents. His mom, Louise, moved with Ted to Tacoma, Washington, where she married a cook named Johnny Bundy in 1951.

Despite his family situation and meager surroundings, he did well in school and was an attractive, polite, well-respected teenager. He was also acutely shy and kept to himself. He eventually graduated with a Bachelor of Science degree in psychology. Then in early 1974 young female college students began to vanish in Washington and Oregon about once a month. Bundy moved to

Serial Killer: Ted Bundy

Salt Lake City in August 1974 for law school, and women began to vanish from Utah—five in just over a month.

Shortly after, hunters discovered bones in a state park, later identified as belonging to two of the missing women from Washington. A few months after that the skulls of four more missing women from Washington and Oregon were discovered on Taylor Mountain. In 1975 three women in Colorado disappeared, followed by another in Idaho and another in Utah.

Ted Bundy was arrested in 1975 for kidnapping and attempted assault in a case where his intended victim managed to escape, and in June 1976 he was sentenced to one to fifteen years in Utah State Prison. In October 1976 he was charged with the murder of a young woman in Colorado. He was extradited to Colorado, served as his own defense attorney, and escaped during the trial. He was recaptured shortly after. Before the trial could conclude, Bundy escaped again and eventually made his way to Tallahassee, Florida, where he killed two girls and injured several others. Still on the loose, he killed again. He was then captured driving a stolen car in Pensacola.

THE DEATH ROW INMATE

Bundy was one of the most charming men you could meet, eloquent and lawyerlike—but inside he was a demon-driven serial killer, rapist, and woman-hater. He told his story to Dr. James Dobson shortly before his execution, saying how at an early age he became addicted to pornography. He also said he had met many killers during his times in prison, and without exception they all had the same addiction.[1]

I didn't know Ted Bundy the killer. I only knew Ted Bundy, the death row inmate. While he only confessed to thirty murders, those who knew Ted Bundy the killer said he may have

DEATH ROW REDEMPTION

killed as many as one hundred young women. One biographer characterized him as "a sadistic sociopath who took pleasure from another human's pain and the control he had over his victims, to the point of death, and even after."[2] Polly Nelson, one of Bundy's attorneys, wrote, "Ted was the very definition of heartless evil," and described him as "a killing machine set loose on society to do the will of a diabolical power."[3]

Bundy was baptized into the Mormon church in 1975, just a few months before he was tried and convicted of kidnapping. The church excommunicated him after his conviction. He was a "professing" Christian toward the latter stages of his life, professing repentance and saying he had received Christ. It is difficult to know—no, it is impossible to know if someone is for real. Many people have asked me if I thought Ted Bundy was really a Christian. I don't know. He did sign his letters "A Brother in Christ." I can't really comment on the genuineness of his professed Christianity.

We exchanged several letters, and Ted did talk about giving his life to Christ. Ted Bundy was executed on January 24, 1989. A couple of years before he was executed, I received this letter from him.

Serial Killer: Ted Bundy

Feb 18, 1987

Thankyou for your lovely card of June 22, 1986, along with the enclosed Lord's Prayer. It showed me that someone cared about me, and for someone in my position that was so important. Please excuse me for taking so long to write you. I hope you can understand that with the number of death warrants signed against me in 1986, I have had a very busy and trying year, and have had difficulty writing to all those who have been kind enough to write.

There is a reason why I am still alive. God is not finished with me yet. Having been born again spiritually, I must now grow to know God's will and love, and to serve Him through His Son Jesus Christ.

Please keep me in your prayers.

in peace

ted

103

Chapter 10

VENGEFUL IRISHMAN: EDDIE FERNCOMBE

O**N THE OTHER** side of the Atlantic, I encountered demons in the life of an inmate.

I made a trip to Ireland in October 1999 to see my newly born-again brother, Eddie Ferncombe. Eddie had a notorious reputation in Ireland. He was well known for his criminal activity. My friend David Berkowitz (aka Son of Sam), who has been a believer since the late 1980s, read an article about Eddie's escapades in Ireland and asked if I would write to Eddie and witness to him as I had done to David many years earlier. New York inmates are not allowed to correspond with other inmates or David would have witnessed to Eddie himself.

Eddie was in the infamous Portlaoise Prison, the maximum-security prison where convicted members of the IRA and other terrorist organizations are held. Security is so tight that it is a no-fly zone and patrolled by a platoon of soldiers who have rifles and anti-aircraft machine guns.

I wrote to Eddie and shared the gospel. He wrote me back saying that if I knew who he really was, I probably would want nothing to do with him. He felt he was too bad for God to love and that surely Jesus couldn't save someone like him. I continued our correspondence, and we became friends. I told him about my family and sent him photos of my dog.

Don Dickerman alongside Eddie Ferncombe (left)

Vengeful Irishman: Eddie Ferncombe

After a few weeks of letters, Eddie accepted Christ by mail. Here is Eddie's story:

I was born in 1972, and as I look back on my life, I never thought I'd reach this far and become the man I am today. Since birth, it seemed I was born to die young from my own self-destruction. So I lived fast and came very close to death many times. Now things are different, Satan's grip on my life is broken, and Jesus Christ is my Savior! The "power" I once knew was violence and crime—that is now gone, along with its pain, anger, hurt, frustrations, blood, sweat, and tears. The Lord and my new Christian friends have helped me break this vicious cycle of self-destruction and harm to others. So what they gave to me, I now give to you, my brothers and sisters, to help inspire hope and change for you also. I give you love and truth.

I could easily blame my childhood for how I turned out, but my brothers and sisters didn't turn out like me. It must have been something else. I was born and reared in a working-class ghetto, riddled with drugs, crime, violence, and youth crime gangs. I witnessed violence at a young age. I came from a broken home. We barely had enough money for food. I have little education, and while my upbringing had some effect on me, I now accept responsibility for my actions, my crimes, and my mistakes. My mother and grandmother raised me since I was two and a half years old. My mom was twenty-five when she had five of us kids. I also have four half-brothers. We moved a lot when I was young, from flat to flat. My mom worked hard to provide for us, and we got lots of love and affection, which is better than material things.

107

I Craved Revenge

Moving around a lot left me to run the streets and hook up with the bad boys. We committed violence as children. I soon learned that my violent ways could be a powerful weapon over people. I loved to hurt people who had done me harm, or had done harm to my family or friends. I never let anyone get away with doing me over. I craved revenge, and I always got it. I was always in trouble in school, expelled often, and eventually at thirteen I was thrown out of school. I never went back.

At this time, I was in and out of the children's court for crimes such as car theft, robbery, and assault. I stole anything I knew I could sell. First it was for drinking; later it was for drugs. I was becoming very violent. Anyone who got in my way, I either stabbed or used hammers or hatchets; it didn't matter. By age fifteen, I had become a professional car thief and burglar, and I had become notorious for stabbing people.

I was a member of a youth crime gang of about forty members, and we controlled the crime in our hood. I was feared by people two or three times my age, and this made me feel powerful. To keep this power, I felt I had to get more violent. The home for troubled kids would not accept me—eventually one did but threw me out for stabbing two people in a fight. At sixteen, I was sent to a youth detention center for twelve months for an assault and for escaping from lawful custody.

While in the detention center, I was in and out of solitary for assaulting inmates and officers. I was only out [of the detention center] for five days when I was arrested for robbery and received another sixteen months for three counts. I was doing drugs pretty heavy at this time. I did this sixteen-month sentence the way I did the first: violence against authority and other inmates. Three months

Vengeful Irishman: Eddie Ferncombe

after this sentence, I stabbed a man to death during a street robbery. I was using heroin, crack, and cocaine, and I was messed up at this time. I was seventeen and had already stabbed twenty-five to thirty-five people, and that doesn't include the others I hurt with other weapons. For the most part, it was rivals that I hurt, those who would have done the same to me.

I was charged with one count of murder at age seventeen. Later this was reduced to manslaughter because of my age and drug dependence. I was given a ten-year sentence. I had always hated authority, so I was in trouble from the start. I wouldn't obey orders from anyone. I assaulted officers and went on all sorts of protests, which caused me to be sent from prison to prison. I was in all of Ireland's prisons and punishment blocks three or four times over. None of this helped. I kept rebelling at any chance because my hate only grew over the many beatings I was given by eight, ten, or twelve guards. In more than eleven years of incarceration, I have only spent about ten months in general population. As the case is now, I spent my time in isolation. Along the way I even dabbled with the occult and have "666" tattooed on me. I had tattoos about hate for everyone, all in my anger for authority.

I hated the system, and the system hated me. I did have the respect of other inmates because I fought the system. I earned my way here to Ireland's toughest prison, housed in the defaulters wing. In 1997, while in the Mountjoy Prison in Dublin, me and five other inmates took five officers hostage. We held them for three days in what has been described as the worst crisis in prison history. We were all sent to the Portlaoise prison, Ireland's most max facility. I am now in a prison within a prison. This is my fourth time here, and three times previously I was on the gangland wing. The guards here wear riot gear any time the doors are opened, and I am always cuffed before leaving my cell and no less than six officers go with me. I received an additional six-year sentence for the siege, and that's why I am on the defaulters wing.

SOMEONE DID CARE FOR ME

Two years ago, I started writing to some Christians, and they showed me love and respect as a human being. They showed me that someone did care for me. They trusted me and took me into their confidence as an equal. This all felt strange to me, as I hated society and thought society hated me, but it also felt good. I wanted what they had. I accepted Christ by mail! I wanted change, I really did, but I did not know God loved me so much that He sent Jesus to save me. Save *me*? I was writing to Don Dickerman in Texas. He sent me the salvation prayer and words of encouragement. I read some of the Bible, and as I said the prayer of salvation...BANG! With tears in my eyes, I began to loudly scream and shout, a feeling of calm came over my thoughts, and I knew something was really happening. The Holy Spirit came into *my* body. Wow!

I wasn't tripping; this was real! Hilary Hughes, a Christian in Dublin, was writing, and John Paul and Aine Hooton from Cork were writing me also words of encouragement. Don sent me some cassette tapes of prison services he conducted in America. As I listened to one of the tapes, he was ministering deliverance to inmates. He bound evil spirits in the name of Jesus, and as he did this on the tape, my body began to get hot and there was stirring inside. It was the middle of winter, and I could not cool off. I stripped to my shorts and I splashed water from my basin in my face. As he commanded spirits to leave, I started doing the same. I knew now I had demons but couldn't find release. I told my chaplain about it the

Vengeful Irishman: Eddie Ferncombe

next day, and he laughed at me. I wrote Don and told him about it, and I asked him to help me. Don told me that when he read my letter, he felt the Lord telling him to come to Ireland and to minister deliverance to me.

That is a day I will never forget. First, he came to see me on Monday to discuss what I needed to do, and he was going to come back on Wednesday to do the deliverance. He talked to me about the necessity of forgiving and that I could not be free until I did. Wow, this was difficult. I had so much anger for the beatings I had taken, for the man who had snitched on me and was now out selling drugs to kids—so much hate! How could I forgive?

He told me it had to be like God forgave me, not based upon them deserving it. He told me to read Matthew 18:23–25. He said, "Forgiveness is not saying what happened is OK. That's not what Jesus said when He forgave me. He didn't say sin's OK. Sin is ugly; it sent Him to the cross. What He said was, I love you anyway. When you forgive, you are not saying what happened is OK. It was painful then, and it is painful now. What you are saying is I wish no harm for you. I want God to love you just like He loves me. If vengeance is in order, I release that to God because He says, 'Vengeance is mine, I will repay, says the Lord' [Rom. 12:19, ESV]. You can do that, Eddie. You have to if I am to help you."

When I left the prison that day and drove back to Dublin, I wondered if Eddie would forgive. I wondered if he could. I knew that my trip would be in vain if he didn't. I prayed for him and asked God for extra measures of grace in Eddie's life. Hilary Hughes, my contact in Dublin, had driven me to Portlaoise and waited while I visited with Eddie. She was not going to be able to drive me there on Wednesday, as I was headed for southern Ireland to preach in a few churches.

On Wednesday I was to be at the prison about 10 a.m. because of the limited one-hour visit and no visits after noon. Well, it was a Murphy's Law day! It seemed everything that could go wrong did go wrong. There was a massive traffic jam. I was stranded in traffic in Dublin, not to mention driving on the left side of the road with the steering wheel on the right. Time seemed to race as I watched the clock and tried to maneuver the roads. It was noon when I finally arrived at the prison. Portlaoise is about thirty miles south of Dublin, and it had taken me almost three and a half hours to drive there.

As I arrived at the prison to visit, others were coming out because visitation was over. I was so discouraged. I had been binding Satan all the way from hindering this visit. I still was expecting victory even though it was not looking good. I explained to the visitation officer that I had come all the way from Texas. "I remember you from Monday, lad. I am going to lunch now. Come back at 1:00, and I will ask the governor [warden] if he will grant you special permission."

I went to get something to eat and prayed for God's intervention during the hour. I remember it was somewhat cool, dreary, and rainy that day. It seemed like the entire ten days I spent in Ireland were that way. I went back to the prison in anticipation of special permission. Surely I would get one hour with Eddie. I was wrong. I got three hours! And I got it in a special area with no one else present. All the visitors had gone, and the officer told me I could have until four o'clock.

I headed back to see Eddie, escorted by a kind Irish officer. He asked me, "Are you like David Wilkerson?" Wilkerson is the well-known founding pastor of Times Square Church in New York and a former street minister.

Vengeful Irishman: Eddie Ferncombe

I knew what he meant. I thought for a minute and said, "Yes. Yes, I am."

The officer said, "You are welcome here, lad!" Look how the Holy Spirit had prepared everything. I wondered now if Eddie had been able to forgive.

BREAKING THE SHACKLES

Eddie's story continues:

> It was a real struggle turning loose of my anger and forgiving those I felt so much hate for. But I realized I must do it because the forgiven must forgive. Those who have received grace must be gracious to others. When I did forgive, I knew something had happened. I knew I was ready for demons to be driven from me. I could hardly wait until Wednesday. When Don came in that day, he told me of many obstacles he had endured that morning. He even arrived too late for visiting time (one hour is all we are allowed). However, in God's plan, because he arrived late and had come from Texas, he was given a three-hour special visit by the governor. The extra time was necessary. I was a little nervous as the time approached. I wasn't sure what to expect. Don said he felt it might be wise to alert the officer who sits in a plexiglass box and observes the visit about the upcoming deliverance. When he told him he was going to be praying deliverance over me, the officer just nodded and said, "'elp yourself, lad. 'elp yourself."
>
> They brought me into the visitation chamber shackled as always. Four officers escorted me. I think Don could tell I was ready to experience deliverance by the look on my face. We talked some and he prayed, acknowledging the Holy Spirit's presence and our need for His direction for me to know complete liberation from the enemy. He

DEATH ROW REDEMPTION

explained to me that when the evil spirits were bound in me that I might very well feel their presence by some kind of manifestation. I already knew that from just listening to the tape.

The name of Jesus Christ is powerful. He explained that demons must have permission to be present through generational curse, abuse, trauma, immorality, occult, and other things. We prayed a prayer, thanking God for salvation and then repenting of unforgiveness, anger, bitterness, hatred, etc., and received the full work of the cross to break the power of any curse.

He also explained to me that while I was previously possessed by demons, I was now possessed by the Holy Spirit of God; that I was redeemed, bought with a price, purchased, God's possession! He explained that the demons were now intruders and their only work now was oppression, that they were in my flesh and soul, not in my spirit. He began to bind the evil spirits in the name of Jesus Christ. I felt all kinds of stirring inside of me, nausea and headache, burning...I became very tensed up.

He began to rebuke spirits and commanded them to leave me. Man, this was some experience! I felt them leaving on my breath, sigh after sigh, release after release, as he commanded spirits to leave—spirits of hate, anger and bitterness, resentments, spirits of rebellion, spirits of murder and death.

For about two hours spirits were leaving me until finally the last one was gone, and I sort of slumped in my seat. The tension was gone, and I felt peace. I remember I felt high—high on God, not drugs. I felt a peace and a calmness I had never felt before. All of my inner battles were gone, all of my hate and my anger, my pain and frustrations. They were all gone, man!

I had always told Don in letters that I could never forgive the system, and some people, never ever! But now,

114

Vengeful Irishman: Eddie Ferncombe

not only could I forgive, I could love. I could truly forgive people, and wow, what a powerful weapon that is. I loved it, and I have never looked back. That was October 26th, 1999, a day I will never forget. The Lord now lives in me, and I feel He is using me to reach others who were and are in my old situation.

I love Jesus so much now. He died for our sins—take time to think about that. I want to make the Lord proud of me and reach as many people as I can. I believe He will open the right doors for me, and I will follow Him without questions. I want all of my Christian friends to be pleased with my life, and I want this testimony to be a big thank you for their love.

My family and my girlfriend have been waiting all of my life for me to truly come home. It won't be much longer now. I have been off drugs totally for over four years, having been a heroin addict for seven, and I have finally beat that. I am now placid, peaceful, and calm; a happy man. The scowl is gone from my face. The hate is gone from my dark eyes, and now they shine. I am hoping this helps anyone who reads it, and I will try to help anyone who writes to me.

Chapter II

TWENTY-FIVE TO LIFE: LAURIE KELLOGG

I N 1992, LAURIE Kellogg's trial for murder garnered national attention because of its emotional, dramatic, and shocking testimony. While a young man named Denver McDowell was the one who pulled the trigger and shot Bruce Kellogg, Laurie was sentenced to twenty-five years to life for murder and manslaughter for her role in the death of her husband.

I met Laurie in the late 1990s when I preached in the Bedford Hills Correctional Institute in New York. I don't remember what I said, but I mentioned something about demons and the occult, and Laurie approached me after the service.

I didn't know who she was at that first meeting, but as I got to know her, I found Laurie to be genuine in her faith. She wasn't a bitter person. She was thankful for her two children and the life she had, but she was probably one of the most abused women I'd ever met while ministering in prisons. Most of the women in prison come from a life of abuse, but Laurie's case was pretty severe.

LOOKING IN THE WRONG PLACES

Laurie described herself as the product of a broken home and much abuse, having experienced sexual abuse at a young age. She had been raised in a Catholic home until about age nine, but she never heard much about Jesus or salvation. After her mom remarried, her family started attending a United Methodist Church, but that lasted only about a year.

By her teen years, Laurie was pretty much on her own. Feeling alone and abandoned, with her mother and stepfather often away, she eventually turned to drugs and alcohol and ended up following the wrong crowd.

In time, her family moved to another state. And that's where she eventually met Bruce Kellogg. She was sixteen, and he was thirty-three. They married and had two children, but their ten-year relationship was filled with abuse.

When I interviewed her in the late 1990s, Laurie told me some of what she endured. She said her husband raped her, beat her to the point that she miscarried, and even sexually assaulted her with a .41-caliber revolver. "I know now that my parents would have done more to get me out of this, [but] I lied to my parents...because I felt that these beatings were a failure on my part," she told me. "I felt that I was not being a good wife because my husband had to beat me.

"If he was angry at me, it was because I had done something wrong or not done something right. And I didn't want my parents to know I was a failure. I left home at sixteen to be with this man, and I felt, as he told me, that I'd made my bed and now I had a lie in it."

She repeatedly made excuses for her bruises: "It seemed I never failed to have any trouble coming up with a story as to why [I had] these bruises: I tripped down the stairs...and slipped over toys and fell in the bathtub and got into more wrestling matches with the kids, where I got the worst of it. I mean, there was always a reason, and he never had anything to do with it—he was never even there. I can't believe I went to such extremes to protect him."

When asked why she didn't leave, Laurie explained: "My entire adult life, I've been imprisoned in one way or another. And I told myself that I could handle this because [abuse] happened all around me. My best friend's [husband], he beat her. She called the police. He beat her twice as bad. I wasn't going to call the police because I knew what the results were. All the other marriages around the neighborhood were breaking up because the women didn't do what was necessary to make their husbands happy. My marriage wasn't going to break up. I'd make it survive. I'd survive my marriage to make my marriage survive. It was such a vicious cycle."

LOSING EVERYTHING

Laurie's life changed forever in 1991 when her husband, Bruce, was fatally shot by eighteen-year-old Denver McDowell. Laurie drove McDowell and three other teens from Pennsylvania to Bruce's cottage in New York. While Bruce slept, McDowell shot him in the head.

Laurie insisted that she had nothing to do with the murder and told me that during the trial she was not allowed to testify about the extent of the abuse she suffered, with the judge telling her, "Mrs. Kellogg, your husband is not on trial. You are." In the end, Laurie was convicted of conspiring to murder her husband and received the maximum sentence.

She lost everything—her husband, who was the only source of stability she had known; her home; her possessions; and her freedom. Worst of all, she was separated from her children.

You might think someone who had suffered so much abuse would be angry at the world. But Laurie wasn't bitter. She told me her heart was full of joy. One night, at her lowest point—when she felt completely alone—she experienced the overwhelming reality of God's love.

She said God reached out to her and told her that He loved her and He always had. She told me it felt as if her eyes were suddenly opened and a heavy burden lifted from her heart. For the first time in her life, she felt truly alive—and loved. That realization changed everything. From then on, she understood her life had purpose and that God had a plan for her.

FINDING PEACE

Laurie found a peace in Christ that nothing else had ever given her. She told me she could now sit across from women in prison and say with confidence, "I've walked in your shoes, and I know the way out." She became a living witness of the love and redemptive power of Jesus Christ to women others had written off as unreachable. Laurie wanted them to see that abuse is not love, and that in Him their lives could be full of love and joy.

Prison was still a dark and evil place, and she admitted that being the kind of witness God wanted her to be was not always easy. The enemy fought her constantly. But her greatest desire was to share with others the wonderful gift of God's love that had so completely transformed her own life.

Laurie prayed the same kind of prayer that I prayed when I accepted Christ, the same prayer that Arnold Munoz prayed, the same prayer that anyone prays when receiving Christ. You can pray it now:

Come into my heart, Lord Jesus, and save my soul. I am a sinner. I need You as my Savior. I believe You are the risen, living Son of God. I confess that I cannot make it to heaven without You. Thank You for saving me. Amen.

One day she told me, "I'm in a maximum-security facility for women, and I experience more freedom every day of my life in here than I experienced when I was home and free and married." Back then, she knew only the bonds of oppression, depression, anger, and fear. Now she knows the joy of the Lord.

121

DEATH ROW REDEMPTION

Laurie was released in 2019 to a New York State halfway house. She is doing well and has taught her two dogs to bow and pray before they get their food. Laurie loves Jesus and is so grateful for her freedom.

HERE YA GO
preacher

DON DICKERMAN
BOX 575
HURST, TEXAS 76053

NORTH BAY, CA 949
PM 1 A
23 JUN 1988

Chapter 12

MASTERMINDED THE MURDER OF HER PARENTS: SHERYL SOHN

"CHRISTMAS NIGHT OF 1980, we had a big family blowout, a terrible argument," Sheryl Sohn told me. "The years and the alcohol had only worsened my mother's attitude toward me. Yet my father and I had only grown closer. That night she gave both me and my father an ultimatum—either I go or she goes."

Sheryl had been coming and going in the home since she was sixteen, and now she felt she had finally established a closeness with her father that was worth keeping. Her life to this point had been filled with disappointment, rejection, pain, and frustration. She was a mature young lady of twenty-two, yet in many ways she was still looking for little-girl love and attention.

She said, "At this point in my life, I felt I had progressed too far in my relationship with my father. I refused to let her come between us again. She had to go! As I mulled it over in my mind, I thought about how much better it would be for both me and my father if she was out of the way. In my mind I must have already killed her every way imaginable. She stole my childhood, my adolescence, my relationship with my father, my memories of my grandmother, and more. Now it was time for her to pay!"

Some of what you are about to read has never been revealed. Of course, Sheryl is terribly ashamed and remorseful for what she has done. However, she has a purpose in revealing this, and it is not money.

DRUGS AND DEMONS

I began to ask around some of my street acquaintances to get the name of someone to kill my mother. I eventually hooked up with a career criminal named Panama Brims.

Masterminded the Murder of Her Parents: Sheryl Sohn

I asked him what he thought about taking out my mother, saying he could have anything he wanted in the house with the exception of the diamond engagement ring my mother wore. It was the last of what my grandmother left to me, and I needed a piece of what could've been and what was mine to hold on to. He thought I was joking at first, but the idea became more and more satisfying as the time passed.

It is hard to express what I was feeling. Obviously, I was not thinking soberly. It just seemed right at the time. When I began to think about how this might affect my father, whom I really loved, I was sure he would find out somehow that I had something to do with it, and the pain would be too much for him. So, in my irrational thinking, I decided to have them killed together. Through it all my father had been loyal to my mother, and he loved her.

On the night of Saturday, December 27, 1980, Sheryl's parents were scheduled to be away from home. That was the night Sheryl would make her mother pay for all the misery she had caused her. Sheryl said, "I really thought I could pull it off, at least the drugs and the demons told me so."

Drugs and demons—where have I heard that before? They go hand in hand, you know. Put your mind in neutral and numb your God-given conscience, and you have extended an open invitation to whatever demons want to control you.

It was all set for that Saturday night when my parents would be gone. I would leave a door open for Panama, he would rob the house, wait for my parents to come home, kill them, get the ring, and get out. He was to keep everything but the ring, meet up with me the next month, and everything would be OK! I even thought there would be a happy ending. That's how deceived I was!

As the time got closer for it to happen, I began to have second thoughts. I was going to a friend's house to spend the night. On the way over to her house, I began to not want it to happen. I thought I had unlocked the door for the preplanned killing, but I hadn't. In my heart I *knew* the door was locked. I guess it was God or my conscience telling me not to go through with it. In the pit of my stomach was an indescribable feeling. I was hoping it wouldn't happen, but I was afraid to call and tell Panama. I knew I couldn't punk out or he would kill me. I was petrified of him! He had told me stories of what he did to people who crossed him in prison.

I met this man when he took an interest in a girl who was, at that time, my best friend. He came around with good cocaine and interesting prison stories. He was both charming and scary, contemplative and impulsive, sensitive and ruthless. He was the kind of guy who would help women with their grocery baskets, tell kids to stay in school, and yet put a gun to the head of a man and pull the trigger without a change in his personality....

I only met this guy two weeks before I asked him to kill my parents. The newspapers called us lovers; actually we were only acquaintances. When I met him and we began to talk, he thought I had nerve. I became his getaway girl, as I drove the car in two of his robberies. I figured Panama would get there, find the doors locked, and leave, forget it for now. But he brought some guys with him, they broke in, ransacked the house, and murdered my parents. I was sound asleep at my girlfriend's house, believing it would not happen.

THE WORST DAY OF HER LIFE

I don't suppose many people who read this will be able to understand what Sheryl is talking about. Feeling that her emotions had been trampled on by her mother for twenty-two years, she would now experience something new—and much worse.

> The worst day of my life was the next morning. Our next-door neighbor's daughter came to get me. She told me my parents were dead! I was in shock; I was so hoping it wouldn't happen. What a fool I was. My heart was about to pound out of my chest as I made my way back to the house.
>
> When I got home, there were police cars everywhere, their flashing lights swirling in the cold morning dampness. There was the district attorney, Ken Gribetz, and the medical examiner, [Frederick] Zugibe. It was like I was stepping into a movie scene. I guess I couldn't accept that it really happened. The next-door neighbors were pointing at me; they were screaming, "Ask her. Ask her what happened. She has to be responsible for this! She's always been a bad seed, always hanging around the wrong people. Ask her!"
>
> Immediately, I was whisked into the house, and I was told I could not go upstairs and see what happened.... Instead they locked me in my room in the basement and wouldn't let me out for three hours. My mind was racing, and every imaginable thought and fear went through my consciousness. Nobody would tell me what happened and what was going on. I beat on the door until I was out of strength. I [plopped] down on my bed in a state of numbness, and I stayed that way for a week.

Sheryl later discovered that her father had been beaten and bludgeoned to death. His entire face and skull had been smashed. It was a brutal scene. The killer intruders had drowned her mother in the bathtub.

A Suspect from the Start

I was arrested just one week after the funeral. I must have been a suspect from the start. Yet, even as they threw me into the squad car, I was numb. I remember the scene well. It was January 15, 1981. I felt nothing. I displayed no outward emotions. There were no feelings. At the time, I had no relationship with reality....

My father was well liked, and he was influential in the town. This led to louder cries for my execution. Friends that I grew up with, neighbors that helped raise me, they all wanted me executed. [New York State has no death penalty.]...It was a typical small community reaction, I'm sure. However, they became a vengeful, bloodthirsty crowd during this pretrial and trial period.

Sheryl received a sentence of twenty-five years to life. Panama Brims received two terms of twenty-five years to life. A second codefendant, James Sheffield, was also convicted of murder. Sheryl Sohn was sent to the women's correctional facility in Bedford Hills, New York. She arrived at the prison in November 1981.

What causes an individual to reach a point where they would even think of murdering their parents? What clouds an individual so much that they prefer darkness to light, a lie rather than the truth?

Sheryl Sohn was born in Manhattan on January 3, 1958, the firstborn child and only daughter of Arnold and Elaine Sohn. What happened to that little baby girl who giggled and smiled back at a mother who nourished, fed, coddled, and changed diapers?

WORTHLESS

Sheryl described her family as a typical lower-middle-class Jewish family when they lived in the Bronx and Queens.

By the time I was in the first grade, my parents wanted to get out of Queens, and we moved to the then-posh Rockland County. It was in this county paradise that I first began to feel like a real person. My parents didn't beat me, but I felt the daily pressure of them having to keep up with the Joneses. My mother was forced to go to work for the first time, and my father had to work two jobs to support our new lifestyle.

I never wanted for food, clothing, or shelter, but I desperately longed for their time! From the confines of my very own bedroom, I would hear my mother's nightly assaults on my father and his inability to provide for her the way she felt that he should have....All the while, to me, he seemed like he was trying the best he could; besides, he was the only one to give me time and attention.

When my father was not around, I began to be the target for Mom's verbal thrashings. She envied the time my father would spend with me and my young brother. Yet, when he was with her, it was constant moaning and complaining. It seemed nobody could ever do anything right for her. I desperately wanted a mom who would take me shopping for school clothes, teach me how to cook, go to Girl Scout meetings with me, and do other girl things....

By the age of nine, it was apparent to me that my mother was jealous of me and my place in the family. She was my grandfather's favorite until I came along, and I was my father's favorite, so that left her out in the cold. My maternal grandfather doted on me, grooming me to be the perfect little lady. I got plenty of compliments

DEATH ROW REDEMPTION

from him and from my father, but the only ones I wanted were from my mother, and they never came, never!

Little by little I would do things to get her attention. By now I figured any attention was better than no attention. I would steal the candy that she would buy especially for guests. I would refuse to clean up my room because I knew it made her mad. It got me attention all right, words that still have deep impressions in my soul. "You're nothing but a fat, worthless pig." "You'll never be anything but a bum." "You can't do anything right." "Why can't you be like your brother?" "I'm sorry I brought you into this world." "You have no respect." "What did I do to deserve such a child?"...

By the time I was eleven, I would not ask for any of my father's time because he suffered so much from my mother when he was with me. When my father would come around, I would pick a fight with him and act out so he would leave me alone, and then he would be spared a verbal onslaught from my mother.

Inside I was so broken that I stayed away from home as much as possible and grabbed on to the affection that I could get from my friends' parents. I was too ashamed to bring friends to my home while my parents were there.... Since nobody was home when I got out of school, I would invite my friends over to impress them...[and] would open up the bar to them and encourage them to drink. I was not even a teenager, but already I was into drugs and alcohol. I was so anesthetized from the verbal abuse of my mother, and I had shut out my father, so I needed an escape from the misery I was feeling. I felt so rejected!

Masterminded the Murder of Her Parents: Sheryl Sohn

THE BLACK SHEEP

Sheryl described herself as the proverbial black sheep. She was only eleven years old, and her self-esteem was on the negative side of zero.

> Outsiders viewed me as a problem child. I guess maybe I even viewed myself that way because I heard it so much. It appeared to others that I was the problem, a bad seed, but I wasn't. I just wanted my mother to love me....
>
> My rebellion became intolerable to my parents. They sought counseling for me because I told them I felt unloved....I began to steal from my mother's pocketbook, and when confronted about it, I would deny it. My rage vented itself in many areas of my life. I began to beat up my younger brother. He knew he was the favorite, and he would rub it in my face. I felt I just didn't fit anywhere....
>
> Things went from bad to worse when I was thirteen. I began to notice hair growth on my face, like a man's. Now I was not only fat and unloved but had hair growing on my face. I always felt I must be some sort of oddity, but this was scaring me....[Cornell University Medical Center] diagnosed me as having cysts on my ovaries that were eating up the female hormones in my body, thus producing an excess of male hormones. This wasn't enough though. Not only was I a fat thirteen-year-old brat with a beard, but every day I heard from my mother how much the medical bills were and how much she was sacrificing for me to get treatment. She told me I was not worth it, and that they would be much better off if I had never been born....
>
> I began to have sex with my girlfriends and began to behave promiscuously. I had my first sex with a boy at age fifteen. We didn't even speak; there were no words at all exchanged. I just thought if maybe I could be the first

of my friends to have sex with a boy, they would envy me, perhaps look up to me.

My so-called friends only hung around me to use me. I was good for drugs and money, to decoy for them, and to help with grades.

When the summer of Sheryl's fifteenth year came around, her grandmother sent her to a diet sleepaway camp. "Because everyone had promised me the world if I would lose weight, I did," Sheryl said. "They always told me I had a pretty face (even with the facial hair), but that losing weight would improve my whole appearance. They said I would have friends, nice new clothes, and the clincher: My mother seemed to like the idea. Maybe this would be the time I would win her love and approval."

SEARCHING FOR LOVE AND AFFECTION

Losing weight was a rude awakening for someone who had always been fat and never even dated a boy. Sheryl came back from camp trim and neat looking. The friends she thought she would gain instead became jealous of her, as boys began to come around and ask her out. "People treat you differently when you are thin. I was still the same person, but my friends tried to make me look foolish; instead of compliments, they would make fun of the hair on my face. I was lonelier than ever."

In her quest for love and affection, Sheryl turned to sex with boys on the football and basketball teams. She began to cut school, steal her mother's car, withdraw money from her bank account, and drive to New York City and just cruise the streets. She was spared much danger during those days. "I just seemed to always barely miss the danger. As soon as I would

Masterminded the Murder of Her Parents: Sheryl Sohn

leave a place, I would hear of someone being shot or the police raiding it."

When she was sixteen years old, Sheryl met a man in a park. He invited her back to his house. What started out as a romantic evening ended in a brutal nightmare. "We had what I called normal sex in his bedroom, and when we finished, he turned from a gentleman to a monster," she said, abusing her in every possible way over and over that night. When the man was through with her, he threw Sheryl out his front door.

"Bloody, cold and wet, alone, and in an alien neighborhood, I made my way through a maze of backyards, fences, barking dogs, and parking lots until I got to a familiar place. I got home just before sunrise." Sheryl didn't have anyone she could tell or turn to for help. She had a very difficult time coming to grips with what was happening in her life. Things never seemed to get better for her, only worse.

> I wanted to change. I tried to get a grip on reality and reform. I was determined to quit school and find full-time employment. School was easy for me; it was too slow for me. I needed something to challenge me; school didn't. I wanted a car, a job, an apartment, and independence....
>
> My grandmother gave me a car...[and] my father got me a job at Bloomingdale's when I was eighteen. He was a furniture salesperson there. But by now I was a loner, totally withdrawn from friends. Nobody wanted to be with the bearded woman of the circus.

Sheryl told me that she didn't have a childhood or an adolescence, so she thought she would try to have a life as an adult. For her, there were no dates, no prom, no parties. "None of my friends were acceptable for my mother," Sheryl said. "[She] only wanted my associates to be wealthy, white, and Jewish. She wanted me to join the yuppies at the country club. She wanted me to socialize with 'the kind that went to the temple.'"

Sheryl thought it absurd that her mother would want her to be with those who went to the temple. They had a Bible in their house; it came from Israel. It was silver and jewel encrusted. It was kept in a velvet sack stored away until the holy days.

> I never recall anyone in my house reading from the Bible, including me. They would just take it out at certain times for company to see and to try to impress people. It was beautiful, but it was always closed.
>
> I used to like to watch biblical movies when they came on TV. I always cried at Jesus movies. I remember asking my father if He was a real person. He told me He was a historical person who was drugged to look like He was dead on the cross, but the plan went awry when a soldier stuck Him with a spear. I didn't know, so I accepted that. When I look back on those movies and how they so touched my heart, I believe it was God revealing His love for me, but I was so steeped in a Christ-denying atmosphere that it slipped on by.

At the age of eighteen, Sheryl finally found a measure of relief. She had a good job, and she was dressing and acting the part of a young woman on her way up the social ladder. However, by now her mother was an alcoholic. The alcohol had always been an influence in her mother's behavior, but it was worse than ever.

Although Sheryl was now a responsible daughter—helping with bills, making certain she did not embarrass her father on the job, helping with chores, and covering up for her mother's drinking—again, things only got worse. Her father had a heart attack, then another. He also had high blood pressure. Sheryl's

Masterminded the Murder of Her Parents: Sheryl Sohn

mother blamed his poor health on Sheryl, and she encouraged her daughter to leave.

At the same time, Sheryl's relationship with her father was stronger than ever, but her mother hated that the two were so close. So once again, to spare her father the abuse, she tried to drive him away. She got involved with a Black man, knowing it would anger her father. "It was a mistake from the start," Sheryl said.

Sheryl left home, and with no place to live, she slept in her car, taking showers at the community college and using public restrooms while maintaining her job. She eventually shared an apartment with her new boyfriend, Ted. After about three years, she discovered he was seeing other women, beating up on them, and even getting one pregnant. When her boyfriend realized that Sheryl knew about the other women, he offered to marry her, but she only wanted out.

With no place to go, Sheryl called home. Her mother would not let her come home, so she found a girlfriend to take her in. She didn't know it, but her father was looking for her. He had overheard the phone conversation and began trying to locate her.

A couple of days later, he found her at her friend's house, and there was a tearful, loving reunion. He encouraged Sheryl to come back home with a promise to keep her mother at bay. He assured her there would be harmony. She was leery—and she was right. From the moment she walked in, it was obvious her mother didn't want her there.

When Sheryl's grandmother died of cancer, her mother even blamed that on Sheryl.

> [My grandmother] left a substantial portion of her inheritance to me with my mother as the trustee until

I reached twenty-five. My mother took everything. She even spent the money to buy my brother gifts, like a car, stereos, and such [even though] he received a sizeable amount of the inheritance himself. The ring that my dear grandmother left for me, the one I cut my first tooth on, my mother took. I was determined to rob her like she was robbing me.

THE SHOOTING GALLERY

Sheryl began to drain her mother's bank account. She forged her signature on checks, stole tax refunds, and sold her fur coats and silver. She used the money to buy drugs, seeking temporary relief from the inner emptiness. Actually, the drugs just created a larger void. She told me she could not understand how a drug could be so powerful that a woman would prostitute herself for a five-dollar bag of China white heroin. She was so intrigued by this that she had to try it.

Some acquaintances took her to what is known as a "shooting gallery" in street vernacular, where intravenous drugs are available.

> The drug made me feel so good I wanted more....We approached what was the rubble of a burned-out building....Upon closer inspection, flanked by two tenement walkups was a metal door with a wood plank in front of it. To get to this door, we actually had to step over a dead man....He was already bloated and stinky. I didn't really want to look but he was the only thing between us and the metal door. Because I wanted this experience so bad, I had to hide my horror and disgust. We climbed over the man and made it through the metal door....This was a poshly decorated apartment with the latest in music technology....These men and women were

Masterminded the Murder of Her Parents: Sheryl Sohn

well dressed and most likely there for a quick fix on their lunch hour. The need for the drug crosses race and economic lines. This gallery was a different crowd with a similar need.

As always, the pain of her life only disappeared momentarily and seemed to come back with greater force. The drugs now controlled her.

Sheryl was a junkie, but her parents did not believe she used the money she stole to buy drugs. They saw no needle marks. They had her tested to verify it. She had lied so much that they didn't know what to believe.

In May 1980 Sheryl entered a drug rehabilitation program, just seven months before her parents were murdered. She progressed to the top of her rank and walked away from the rehab after three months. She used a pay phone to call her father, and he picked her up and brought her home. Before Sheryl got home with her father, her mother had already called the rehab facility and told them he would bring her back immediately. But her father put his foot down and made sure there was no quarreling. He insisted Sheryl be treated with respect.

However, the effects of age and alcohol had only worsened her mother's attitude. Then came the events of Christmas 1980, which resulted in the murder of Sheryl's parents and Sheryl's conviction for murder.

SURRENDER AND A BIRTHDAY

Sheryl was placed in the Rockland County Jail. Inmates refused to speak to her. She had no money and no one to help her, and the jail had no provisions for female inmates. The warden purchased underwear and hygiene items for her. She was all alone, and no one cared. In the midst of all the hate mail and silence from other inmates, she began to get cards and letters from an inmate at another prison. He told her, "Jesus loves you, Sheryl. Jesus died for murderers, He died for sinners, and He lives today to forgive you and receive you." However, at the time, she dismissed him as a Jesus freak.

Sheryl was in the county jail for eleven months. Out of boredom, she attended a fellowship meeting hosted by some Christian women who came into the jail to minister.

> I went to their classes, and I really enjoyed their warmth. I even read the scriptures they left and tears came in my eyes, but the memories of what I had been taught about Jesus kept me from yielding.
>
> The conviction and drawing of God's Holy Spirit was really bothering me, so much so that I quit going for a while. Those feelings in the pit of my stomach kept bugging me, so I didn't go. But the feeling and the drawing didn't stop. The Holy Spirit was a stranger to me then, but today He is a dear friend and constant companion. It was as if He would pick me up and make me go to those meetings.
>
> No doubt I got more hugs and felt more love than at any time in my entire life. Those Christians didn't condemn me; they didn't force anything on me; they just loved me and told me about Jesus. Still, I couldn't commit. I wanted to, but my Jewish background, intellectualism, and the overwhelming feeling of unworthiness would not let me. So they brought out the heavy artillery...a little Jewish grandmother who was a Christian! She was in her sixties and had only been saved about ten years. This woman generally did not do prison ministry, but she came this day on a mission. The others had told her about me and my Jewish background.
>
> Grandma Frieda (I still call her that) and I had a long talk. Before she left that night, I had accepted Jesus Christ

Masterminded the Murder of Her Parents: Sheryl Sohn

as my personal Savior. I raised my arms in surrender to the one who loved me so much that He gave His life for me. In tears I made my confession unto salvation! I still didn't feel worthy of love. I certainly didn't understand how the Creator of all there is could take time for me, much less that He could love me. But I had an inner peace that made me know that He did.

On August 27, 1981, Sheryl had a birthday. She was born again. She was received into the kingdom and born into the family of God.

I began to read my Bible daily, and I prayed daily. My life was changing daily also. The cursing began to go, then it was gone. My craving for drugs was gone. Gone! I felt deep remorse, sincere heartfelt regret over what I had done. I felt sorry for my codefendants....I forgave them, and I prayed they would forgive me for getting them involved. I was responsible. I put the idea in their heads.

As sorry as I felt for my deeds and my sins, I still could feel nothing for my mother. I grieved for my father for years....It took me three years to realize I didn't hate my mother. I loved her so much that I could not deal with her not loving me. Now I can look back and see how Satan had deceived me and had used all of those circumstances to destroy my family and me.

Sheryl arrived at the state prison for women in Bedford Hills, New York, on November 24, 1981. She had been saved only three months but had grown considerably in her new life. She was learning to depend upon God's Word and the leadership of His Holy Spirit. She had found God's mercy and grace while in the county jail, but now she was in prison.

They were waiting for me when I arrived at Bedford Hills. Inmates know—somehow they always know—who is coming and all about their crimes. There is an unwritten code among inmates. Certain crimes are not tolerated, such as rape, baby killing, child molestation, and now patricide, my crime.

I was bombarded with threats—newspaper articles with nasty pictures drawn on them and messages written on them. Name calling and personal invitations to fight were as regular and predictable as count time [when activities stop and inmates are physically counted four or five times daily]....

The inmates who wanted to do violence to me slowly changed. I just loved them. I was no punk, but I didn't provoke them. They saw that I was a stand-up person, and they perceived that I could forgive them. They began to come to me for help with reading or writing. Many of my antagonizers were becoming friends over a period of time. God was merciful to me. He still is.

Sheryl Sohn was a fixture in the chapel. She was always there, and it was there that I met her. She had written her name on a sheet of paper, along with some other ladies who requested literature and correspondence from our ministry. When I returned to Texas and scanned the list of names, I noticed her prison number indicated she had arrived in 1981. Most of the others were only a few months or weeks old, while hers indicated she had been there for ten years. I wrote her a letter telling her I loved her and that I was aware she had been there a long time. Here is a portion of the letter I received back from her.

Masterminded the Murder of Her Parents: Sheryl Sohn

Dear Brother Don,

Praising our God for his goodness, greatness and grace... and your wonderful compassion. I was so moved by your simple letter of tender thoughtfulness that I had to put everything down and write to you immediately! To begin, let me tell you what a blessing your services are. The Holy Spirit always moves so quietly and softly when you come.... What a pleasure to hear the whisper of God's Holy Spirit speaking directly to your heart. You're right, I have been here a long time...Nov. 24, 1981 to be exact....Man says that I still have 15 years to do for the double homicide of my parents...which, sadly, I masterminded. I believe God has given me a ministry to the Jew and the intellectual.... Brother Don, I want to encourage you in your ministry to the inmates. I pray he open even more doors for you to go in with the light of the gospel. I pray he will raise up supporters for you financially....God Bless!

Sheryl

1 Corinthians 15:58

In spite of her dark past, Sheryl Sohn escaped from darkness by the mercy and grace of Jesus Christ. She has learned that God is her source and her resource.

Many days were spent in hunger. Many nights my companions were silent tears. But they have led to a development in my faith, and He has been faithful to meet my needs. While I get no visits and no packages, no trailer visits, God continually provides for my needs. He grants me favor with people and blesses the work of my hands. The greatest blessing of all is that He has allowed me into His army. He accepted me. He took me just like I was.

141

Now I am qualified to suffer for Him; in doing so, I know His resurrection power.

Jesus Christ is not only the head of my life, but the toes, the hands, the legs, the feet, the ears and eyes; He is my everything. I am exuberant about my relationship with Jesus, and I'm not ashamed to say so. He has made me a part of a royal family and has given me His divine nature. I am welcome in the family! I love Him. I love Jesus. My God is truly an awesome God!

Chapter 13

THE MAN WHO SHOT JOHN LENNON: MARK DAVID CHAPMAN

I HAVE BEEN IN many prisons over the years. I have vivid memories of some, but others just run together since they are all pretty much alike—numbers instead of names, barbed wire and bars, rules, and hours of isolation and loneliness. They all sort of blend together with the common theme: locked up and lonely.

Some prisons stand out because of their reputations—prisons like Attica Correctional Facility in New York. You may remember the stories about the Attica prison riot. Inmates rioted over conditions in the prison, including overcrowding, physical abuse, unfair visitation policies, and poor medical care. The prisoners took forty-two staff members, both corrections officers and civilian employees, hostage and gained control of the prison. Forty-three people died, including thirty-three inmates and ten prison employees, and all but four of those were killed by law enforcement when the governor gave the order to retake the prison. No other US prison uprising has had more fatalities. That certainly makes Attica stand alone as a prison with one of the worst reputations.

I have been to Attica many times. I receive a lot of mail from inmates, and one day I had a stack of letters on my desk. One of my sons looked at the top letter in that stack of unopened mail. He said, "Dad, do you know who that is? That's the man who shot John Lennon!"

Actually, I didn't know that. I read his letter with piqued interest.

Don Dickerman praying with Mark David Chapman

Mark David Chapman said he had seen our newsletter and felt impressed to write. He asked if I could come visit him. I knew his great chaplain, Chaplain Carter, and I wrote to him to arrange a visit. Mark was inside the prison but housed in a separate building for his protection. He was a marked man. I met with Mark and discovered he has a unique story.

Born in Fort Worth in 1955, Mark grew up with a military father and a mother who was a nurse. He joined the Boy Scouts, tried going to Sunday School, and didn't get into serious trouble. But it was the sixties, the hippie movement was in full swing, and at fourteen he began using drugs and listening to rock music.

For two years he searched for happiness in all the places he knew to look, but something was always missing. At 2 o'clock one morning after a rock concert, he was arrested just a block from his home, and when his father came to pick him up, Mark saw him cry for the first time in his memory. This had an impact on him.

MEETING JESUS

A friend invited Mark to a weekend getaway with his church at a youth camp in northern Georgia. That night by the lake, they showed a film about knowing Jesus. Like everyone he knew, Mark believed in Jesus, but as a historical figure, not as someone who wanted to actually know him. He felt sure a religious experience wasn't for him. Still, there was something different about this Jesus in the film, and it intrigued him.

One unforgettable night Mark was alone at his grandmother's house in Daytona Beach, Florida. He was out of drugs, friendless, and lonely. There seemed to be no purpose to his life. As he lay on the living room sofa, he reached his hands

DEATH ROW REDEMPTION

toward heaven with his eyes closed, grasping desperately for the hope he had heard about that could replace his pain. He said, "Help me. If You're there, come to me." Suddenly, in that room, he met Jesus. "He came," Mark told me. "He forgave me, and I began to walk with Him." It hadn't taken any special religious experience at all. He simply called out to Jesus, and He answered. Jesus was real, and Mark knew He had accepted him.

Yet Mark gradually fell back into old patterns. Though he didn't start using drugs again, life went on as usual. He graduated from high school, moved a couple of times, and eventually forgot about God altogether.

Depression swallowed Mark like a black cloud. Stuck in a dead-end job and severely depressed, he sold his things, bought a one-way ticket to Hawaii, and made plans to end his life. He rented a car, found a quiet place on the coast, hooked a cheap vacuum cleaner hose to the car's exhaust pipe, and sat inside with the engine running, glad everything would soon be over.

His plan failed, and sometime later he was awakened by a concerned fisherman. "I saw the mercy of God in that a hole had been burned through [the hose], so I wasn't getting all the [carbon monoxide]," he said. "And I just said, 'Wow...God wants me to stay alive.'"

Terrified by what he had tried to do, he drove back down the highway, seeking help. He found his way to a hospital and was admitted to its psychiatric unit, where he slept for three days.

Under their care, his depression lifted, and he eventually got a job at the hospital as a housekeeper. He made plans to achieve his goal of traveling around the world, and about a year later he succeeded. But although he felt like he was back on his feet, he was still deeply in need of help.

KILLING JOHN LENNON

Mark started getting depressed again, but he was also becoming confused and paranoid. One day, while at the library in Honolulu, he came across a book called *John Lennon: One Day at a Time*. In it, he saw pictures of Lennon in an exclusive condominium. "I took what he was doing as hypocrisy when all along I was probably the bigger hypocrite," Mark told me. "I got angry that he was living in this splendor when he had sung about peace and about love."

One night, as he sat alone in his apartment, he looked at the book and then at his copy of The Beatles's *Sgt. Pepper's Lonely Hearts Club Band* album, and the idea of murdering Lennon suddenly entered his mind. He soon became obsessed with killing him.

Twice in two months, Mark left his home in Honolulu to go to New York City. He was on a mission to destroy John Lennon, whom he felt had betrayed him, but the first time, he changed his mind and returned home. He had a gun and was prepared to do it. But he couldn't go through with it.

The second time, he would not fail. He arrived at LaGuardia Airport the morning of December 6, 1980, having packed the gun in his luggage, and got a room a ten-minute drive from the famous Dakota building on West 72nd Street, where John and Yoko Lennon lived.

His mind was consumed with a diabolical plan, and he was there to carry it out. An inner voice still told him to go home and forget it; another voice insisted, "Do it. Do it."

Someone had told Mark that if you wanted Lennon's autograph, get one of his albums and he would sign it. When he approached him, John Lennon took the *Double Fantasy* album he held out, motioned to him for a pen, and wrote "John

Lennon, 1980." The revolver was heavy in Mark's coat pocket, but he couldn't bring himself to reach for it. Lennon smiled, handed the album back, and asked, "Is that all you want?"

He muttered, "Thanks, John," and watched Lennon walk away. The voice screamed at him, telling him he was a coward, a failure who had missed his chance at greatness. On the other hand, he was pleased to have John Lennon's autograph and told himself that should be enough. Maybe he should just go back to Hawaii and forget the whole thing. But the voice still haunted him: "Do it. You're here. Just do it."

He stayed. He was waiting when John Lennon and his wife returned to the Dakota in their limousine at eleven o'clock that night. The back door of the limousine opened, and Yoko got out. She walked up the driveway and under the archway toward the steps. John Lennon climbed out of the limousine. Mark thought Lennon recognized him, and he didn't smile. He walked past Mark and hurried under the archway after Yoko. His back was to Mark, and the voice inside said, "Do it! Do it! Do it! Do it! Do it!" Mark aimed at Lennon's back and pulled the trigger five times.

"I just stood there," Mark told me. "And the doorman came running over to me with this look on his face, utter shock.... And he said, 'What have you done? What have you done?' And I said, 'I just shot John Lennon.'"

The doorman shook the gun from his hand and kicked it across the driveway. It took two minutes for the police to arrive, but Mark didn't try to leave the scene. "I just didn't have a place to go," he said. "I mean, that was it for me. That was the end."

On the night of the murder, he slumped in the back seat of a police car, terrified, as police and emergency workers swarmed over the scene. The death of John Lennon was no one's fault but his own. He wasn't on drugs. He wasn't the crazed fan some people tried to label him in an effort to understand. He had become so lost inside himself, so self-deluded, so desperate, that he tried to become somebody by ending the life of a man he didn't even know.

NOT THE SAME

Today he is not the same Mark David Chapman. He has the Lord Jesus Christ. He knows he is not perfect, but he is close to the Lord now, and he finally understands why he did what he did and the grief it caused. He still grieves over what he has done, but the thing that keeps him going is Jesus Christ. Without Him, Mark knows he would be dead.

I asked him if he had a final comment for anyone who may be in the grips of darkness and doesn't know how to get out. Here's his reply:

> One word: Jesus. If you have Jesus in your life and you want Him in your life, He'll take you in. He'll love you and show you that you don't need anything else; you don't need Satan. You don't need things of the world that you thought were so great that just ended you up in prison or worse. You don't need anything but Him....
>
> You come to God in whatever way you want to. You don't have to be on your knees. You don't have to go into an elaborate church. It can happen on the floor of your cell, underneath your bed. It doesn't matter where you're at. You come to God and say, "Forgive me for these things. I want to find You. I want You in my life."

Chapter 14

THE HILLSIDE STRANGLER: KENNETH BIANCHI

THE WASHINGTON STATE Penitentiary was built in 1886, and the first inmates arrived in 1887. The prison is sometimes called Walla Walla, after the town where it is located; "the Walls" by inmates; or "the Pen" by locals in the area. It was the location of Washington's death row until the Washington Supreme Court ruled the death penalty unconstitutional in 2018.

Ken Bianchi, known as the Hillside Strangler, now lives in that prison.

CRIMINAL PARTNERSHIP

Bianchi's birth mother was a prostitute who gave him up for adoption when he was two weeks old. He was adopted by Nicholas and Frances Bianchi of Rochester, New York. He was deeply troubled, even as a child. He was of above-average intelligence, but he did not live up to his potential. His adoptive mother used terms such as "lazy" and "compulsive liar" to describe him. When he was ten, he was diagnosed by a psychiatrist as having passive-aggressive personality disorder. Bianchi's adoptive father died suddenly when he was thirteen.

Shortly after he graduated from high school, Bianchi married his high school sweetheart, but the marriage was short-lived and ended in under a year. He enrolled in college, planning on becoming a police officer, but he dropped out after his first semester. A series of menial jobs led to a security guard position at a jewelry store, where he began stealing.

In 1976 Bianchi moved to Los Angeles, where he started spending time with his cousin Angelo Buono. The two formed a criminal partnership, initially working as pimps, which ranks as one of the lowest human crimes in my book. By October

The Hillside Strangler: Kenneth Bianchi

1977, the cousins escalated to murder when, while posing as police officers, they beat, sexually assaulted, and strangled a prostitute. It was the first of a series of murders that became known as the Hillside Strangler murders, as the police thought one man was committing the crimes. Up until Bianchi's arrest in January 1979, Bianchi and Buono sexually assaulted, tortured, and murdered ten young women and girls, the youngest being only twelve years old.

Bianchi actually applied for a job with the Los Angeles Police Department and even went on ride-alongs with officers as they searched for the Hillside Strangler, not knowing one of the men they were looking for was in the back seat. When Buono found out about the ride-alongs, he threatened to kill Bianchi if he didn't move away. Bianchi moved to Washington, where he killed the last two victims of the Hillside Strangler, although without the help of his partner. Because of clues left at the crime scene, the police identified him and arrested him the day after the last two murders.

When he was tried for his crimes, Bianchi pleaded not guilty by reason of insanity. He initially tried to fake multiple personality disorder, but once his claims were challenged by psychiatrist Martin Orne and evidence, including multiple books on psychology and the source of the name of his fake second personality, he eventually admitted to faking the disorder. He changed his plea to guilty to avoid being sentenced to death. Bianchi was sentenced to six life sentences with the possibility of parole. He was denied parole in 2010, but he is eligible to apply for parole again in 2025. Angelo Buono, his partner in crime, was also tried and convicted. He was sentenced to life in prison, and he died in prison in 2002.[1]

Bianchi told me in several letters that he had genuinely

153

DEATH ROW REDEMPTION

repented and accepted God's amazing grace. He also said that he read and studied his Bible. As of this writing, Kenneth Bianchi is still in Walla Walla prison in Washington.

Chapter 15

THE MONSTER:
WILLIE BOSKET JR.

EADLINES FROM *THE New York Times* in 1989 included:

A Boy Who Killed Coldly Is Now a Prison "Monster"[1]

Jailed "Monster" Gets More Prison Time for Stabbing Guard[2]

Caged for Life, and His Jailers Stand Back[3]

The first article began, "Willie Bosket, a self-proclaimed 'monster' whose five-year sentence for two subway murders when he was 15 years old led New York to toughen its juvenile criminal laws, will be sentenced this morning for his latest crime, stabbing a prison guard."[4] The second noted that Willie Bosket, "who once admitted committing more than 2,000 crimes by age 15, including the two murders and 25 stabbings, maintains that he is a 'monster' created by the criminal-justice system."[5] Another article refers to Bosket as "the murderer who is considered New York State's most violent prisoner."[6]

Willie Bosket Jr. had the reputation as one of the most dangerous inmates in America. After he was convicted for the 1989 stabbing of a prison guard, Bosket was housed in solitary confinement "in a specially-built plexiglass-lined cell stripped of everything but a cot and a sink/toilet combination, with four video cameras watching him at all times."[7] He was also written up for almost 250 disciplinary infractions in less than a decade.[8]

However, Dr. Hector Chiesa, the prison chaplain, told Willie that God loved him.

I'm not sure if Willie had ever heard those words. Dr. Chiesa continued to visit Willie and just love him with the love of Christ Jesus. One day the most dangerous man to ever be locked in a New York prison asked Jesus to come into his heart and forgive him, to be his personal Savior. That was many

The Monster: Willie Bosket Jr.

years ago. Willie is saved today. I know Willie Bosket Jr. I have seen his plexiglass cage, and we have prayed together. I interviewed Willie in prison. Here is a portion of the transcript.

> DON: Willie, the *National Enquirer* and *Time* magazine have described you as a human monster, a cold-blooded, heartless killer. How would you describe yourself?

> WILLIE: I sincerely describe myself as a loving, kind, and compassionate human being, concerned about those issues of oppression by the powerful over the downtrodden in America and abroad.

> DON: What do you think made you as you are? Would you say you were born mean? Did some set of circumstances influence your makeup?

> WILLIE: No, I was not born mean. I truly do not consider myself mean at all. However, because of the trials and tribulations in my life as a ghetto child growing up in extreme squalid conditions of poverty and oppression in Harlem, and spending all of my life from age nine in juvenile reformatories, psychiatric wards, and adult prisons, observations and experiences have given me much knowledge, wisdom, and understanding about certain realities concerning those issues that affect the downtrodden in society and remains in the darkness of social apathy and unconcern. When one can see the illumination of those realities, it does not usually make one very happy.

> DON: You have only lived outside of prison for three years since you were nine—your parole date is 2062. What hope do you have, and what will you try to accomplish in prison?

WILLIE: I truly try not to, and don't live or exist, on hopes. I can't remember ever doing that in life. I guess, to me, living for hopes is to ignore what is and is not. I try to deal with what life has in store for me, no matter what that is. I guess you could say that I trust the power of Almighty God to guide me towards the chosen ultimate purpose for my life. I try not to dictate life.

Basically, while in prison or out of prison, I will endeavor to accomplish making contributions toward eliminating the perpetuation of evil and oppression, and to leave a legacy for our children so that they may never have to know the pains and sufferings I have known.

DON: Having seen where you must live, I must ask this question. Is your punishment just? What do you think the State of New York should do to you?

WILLIE: No, the punishment is not just and cannot even be considered anything but a manifestation of penal regress to those times before the Attica riot and the move towards prison reform here in America. The punishment against me is the system's intention to nullify the threat I am to the system by using medieval and barbaric conditions of solitary confinement to cause irreparable psychological, emotional, and physical harm to me towards my eventual demise. It is not necessarily a question of what the State of New York should do *to* me, but they should have done *for* me as a nine-year-old child in their custody and care.

Right now, I think the State of New York should accept my offer to cooperate with a serious study of me towards insight and understanding of what makes Willie Boskets and be able to prevent future Willie Boskets.

DON: You were born in the drug capital of New York and grew up in abject poverty. If you had been born in

The Monster: Willie Bosket Jr.

Sherman, Texas, in a middle-class white family, like I was, would things be different?

WILLIE: Don, candidly speaking, Jesse Jackson and I may have been running partners for the presidency and vice presidency of the United States.

DON: Something dramatic happened in your life. Rev. Dr. Chiesa, our mutual friend, told you about Jesus and God's great love. What happened?

WILLIE: To explain what happened is, in a way, so simple. But then again, it's so complicated. One must know a little about Dr. Chiesa first to understand what happened. Dr. Chiesa gave me, showed me, and shared with me a love and friendship and loyalty in my most desperate time of need that I have always expected to find from a true friend, only to find disappointment so many times. Dr. Chiesa gave me an unconditional love and friendship and loyalty and constantly told me that his love was a reflection of God's love. Well, I truly couldn't resist wanting to know more about the God that was responsible for this beautiful man. Everything else is history and history in the making.

DON: How has Jesus made a difference in your life, Willie?

WILLIE: I have found a peace, a happiness, within myself so profound that I truly cannot find the words to express.

DON: The Bible calls this "peace that passes all understanding" [Phil. 4:7]. The skeptics will call it jailhouse religion. What do you say to those who will say you are just playing a game?

WILLIE: A true believer and knower of God knows there is no such thing as playing games with God. So anyone who skeptically calls it a game is of no concern to me because they have much to learn about God. I truly believe they are under the impression that to accept Christ is to be submissive, passive, and ultimately defenseless against the oppression and brutality against them. Not so! With Christ, we are able to fight harder, stronger, and more effectively. I'm still a revolutionary and will always be one. But now I am a revolutionary ambassador for God, in God's army. Praise God! God does not say that we have to abandon our struggles for freedom, justice, and equality. We can and must continue to struggle against evil. But the struggle is much more effective when you are protected by an undefeated army.

DON: God bless you, Willie. I am happy for your new-found peace in Christ and the eternal life you now have because of Jesus, His mercy and grace. I hope to see you again soon.

LEGACY OF VIOLENCE

Willie Bosket Jr. was born in Harlem in 1962. Several months before his birth, his father, Willie Sr., killed two men and was sentenced to life in prison for the crime. While Willie Sr. was eventually released, he was imprisoned again for molesting his girlfriend's daughter. His girlfriend helped him escape from prison, but when the police caught up to them, Willie Sr. shot his girlfriend and then himself to avoid capture.

To say that Willie had a traumatic childhood would be a gross understatement. Willie's father was not the only one with a criminal record. Willie's grandfather was imprisoned for kidnapping and sexually assaulting a child. When Willie's

The Monster: Willie Bosket Jr.

grandfather was released from prison, Willie became the victim of his repeated abuse. Evidence of Willie's troubled childhood included actions such as attacking his sister, skipping school, stealing cars, picking pockets, assaulting medical personnel, and arson. Willie was smart and could be charming, but no one seemed to be able to help him or deal with his behavior—his mother, teachers, administrators, social workers, judges, doctors, or psychiatrists.

Starting from the age of nine, Willie was in and out of several juvenile detention centers and reform schools. Then in 1978 Willie murdered a man on the subway while robbing him of a gold watch and a ring. Over a ten-day period starting with that murder, Willie—sometimes accompanied by his cousin—robbed multiple people on the subway, murdering a second victim and seriously injuring another. Willie pleaded guilty to two counts of murder and one count of attempted murder for the crime spree. The prosecutor in the case said, "I think he was the most violent offender that I had ever come across in twenty-five years as a prosecutor."[9] Willie was given the maximum sentence—five years in a youth detention center.

Three months after his release from the detention center, Willie was arrested again, this time for assault and attempted robbery. That was in 1983. Willie was sentenced to seven years in prison for that crime, but he has never been released, as his crimes while in prison—including stabbing the guard, other attacks on guards, setting fires, and attempting escape—have added decades to his sentence. And Willie has spent decades in solitary confinement in the specially designed plexiglass cell.[10]

According to the New York Department of Corrections and Community Supervision, Willie won't be eligible for parole until September 16, 2062, about three months before his one hundredth birthday.[11]

I recall asking Willie why he was always trying to stab and injure officers. I was surprised at his answer: "It's the only voice I have. If I get sent to court and can talk and tell my story, if I get a newspaper to listen—it's the only voice I have."

I mentioned that Willie had almost 250 disciplinary infractions. They occurred from 1985 to 1994. However, he has not had a disciplinary violation since. It is amazing how Jesus makes a difference!

When I went to Woodbourne Correctional for services, Dr. Chiesa told me about Willie. He took me to the warden's office, and we requested permission for me to see Willie. The warden initially said that he was not allowed any visits and the officers were not allowed to speak to him, but we were eventually given permission to see Willie.

We left the warden's office, and Dr. Chiesa said, "Follow me." He started up the staircase to the fifth floor. As we opened the door, immediately to our right was the cage they built to contain the "monster." Dr Chiesa introduced me, and that began a relationship. Willie was supposed to die in that cell. However, after many years of complying with all the rules, he was transferred back into the general population at the Wende Correctional Facility near Buffalo. He is even able to communicate through an email system unique to New York prisons. I received this email from him. Willie is not the "monster" he once was.

Brother Don:

Really hope you've been well these past years.

The Monster: Willie Bosket Jr.

A real quick note hoping you'll respond as soon as possible.

I was released from solitary confinement ("the box"). I am not as you remember me the last time we met with each other. I am now in general prison population at Wende Correctional Facility near upstate Buffalo, New York.

I would love to get an email from you soon....Hope to hear from you soon. God bless you! Thanks for sharing Jesus and being my friend.

IN CHRIST LOVE
WILLIE

Chapter 16

CULT LEADER:
CHARLES MANSON

DEATH ROW REDEMPTION

CHARLES MANSON WAS an infamous cult leader. His so-called "family" committed at least nine murders in the late 1960s, and they are suspected of several more. Before the murder spree, Manson had spent more than half his life in reform schools and prisons. His known crimes included armed robbery, auto theft, forgery, and sexual assault.

Manson was sent to the California state prison in 1971 after being found guilty of seven counts of first-degree murder along with one count of conspiracy to commit murder in the 1969 deaths of Abigail Anne Folger, Wojciech Frykowski, Leno and Rosemary LaBianca, Steven Earl Parent, Sharon Tate Polanski, and Jay Sebring. Sharon Tate Polanski, a Golden Globe–nominated actress, was eight months pregnant at the time of her murder. Manson was convicted later in 1971 of two more counts of first-degree murder for the deaths of Gary Hinman and Donald Shea. He was initially sentenced to death, but when the California Supreme Court ruled that the death penalty was unconstitutional, his sentence was changed to life imprisonment.

Manson applied for parole twelve times, but he was never granted it. He died of natural causes in 2017.[1]

I had been going into prisons for a few years when I heard of Charles Tex Watson, a member of the murderous "family" led by Charles Manson, becoming a Christian. I knew who he was, but I did not know him personally. He was born and raised in the McKinney area of Texas. I wrote to him, and we became friends by mail. He wrote to me for several years, and he certainly seemed genuine.

To let you know what others thought about Tex Watson's salvation, I want to include a letter from singer Pat Boone, who performed at his prison in San Luis Obispo. Pat is responding to a query he received about Manson's "family."

166

Cult Leader: Charles Manson

Friday, November 11th, 1977

Dear Pat:

Every now and then, I read something about Charles Manson. I know he's cooling his heels in prison (thank God), but what's happened to his "disciples," the ones who actually did the killing of Sharon Tate and her friends? Have they been executed?

—Bayron Binkley

No, they haven't been executed. But a couple of them have died—and been raised from the dead.

I'm talking about Charles "Tex" Watson and Susan Atkins. Under the hypnotic influence of "Jesus-Satan" Charles Manson and all kinds of mind-bending drugs, these two young people led the pack to the Tate and LaBianca homes and brutally slashed helpless people to death. They were found guilty and sentenced to life imprisonment.

Many felt this was too good for them, and that if there was ever an open-and-shut case for capital punishment, this was it. But—end of story. Right?

Wrong.

Recently I visited the huge, sprawling California Men's Colony where as many as 2,000 major offenders are imprisoned, close to San Luis Obispo, in central California. I was there at the invitation of Chaplain Ray to do a show for the inmates and to participate in a prison-wide spiritual outreach. Almost 509 prisoners had jammed into the big recreation hall to hear the music, and excitement was high. The fellas there don't get much in the way of entertainment, so this was a big day.

It was over 90 degrees as I arrived backstage, so I took

167

DEATH ROW REDEMPTION

off my jacket and looked around for someplace to put it—when a tall, lean young man smilingly reached out to take it from me.

"Let me help you, brother Pat: praise the Lord!" He looked at me with clear blue eyes and an open, joyful expression. "I'm the chaplain's assistant, Charles Watson."

"Charles Watson? Not 'Tex' Watson—?" I was obviously taken aback, to put it mildly.

"Yeah, that's me," he answered, still smiling, "but I don't use the 'Tex' anymore. I'm just Charles—brother Charles."

And I couldn't help it. As I looked deep into those eyes, my mind instantly flashed to the pictures I'd seen of the Tate house and the accounts of the terrible atrocities this man had committed. I thought, "Sharon Tate looked into these very eyes and begged for mercy, for herself and her unborn child. And found none. These were the last eyes she saw, and filled with drugs and mindless malevolence, they sentenced her to gory death."

Why wasn't I repulsed? Why didn't I have cold chills? Why did I find myself warmly shaking his hand, returning his smile, actually liking him?

Because these eyes were different now. There was no hate there, no cold haze, no demonic menace; there was openness, an honest warmth, an obvious and earnest desire to communicate friendship. Naturally, I was intrigued and I asked Charles what had happened.

"Brother Pat, I met Jesus. That's all. Right here in prison, after the trial and after the drugs all wore off, and after I finally saw what I'd been part of and what I'd done, and the way I'd let the Devil use me, I fell on my knees and asked God to forgive me. I asked Jesus to forgive me and come into my heart—and He did. He can't take away or change what I did, but He's changed me. I've been born again!"

The prisoners were beginning to stomp their feet and

Cult Leader: Charles Manson

whistle impatiently from out front, so still a little numb from this encounter, I started the show. About midway through the program, the power went off.

The recreation hall was plunged into semi-darkness, there was no sound system, the air-conditioning ceased, and there was going to be a very uncomfortable, indefinite delay. Immediately the inmates were hooting and rattling their chairs, and the guards were considering marching them back to their cells, sensing a possible riot.

Suddenly a voice cut through the darkness, high and strong, singing "Amazing Grace, how sweet the sound, that saved a wretch like me...." The noise subsided, while some of the prisoners began to sing along. There was something contagious, something appealing about the voice and the "rightness" of singing just then. "I once was lost, but now I'm found; was blind, but now I see."

I peered through the shadowed hall to see who the song-leader was. It was Charles Watson.

For almost 20 minutes he led the inmates in singing, and though not all joined in, the mood was tempered and the situation was calmed until the power was hooked up again, and the show could go on. Chaplain Ray told me later that the change in Charlie is dramatic and total. One of the guards shook his head in amazement and said, "A lot of the cons think this is some kind of act with Watson, some effort to get out. They make it mighty tough on him, but he just smiles and keeps going. No doubt about it, it's real."

And then, just a few days ago, I got a letter and a picture from Susan Atkins, the girl who participated with Watson in carrying out Manson's bloody directives.

I'd read reports of her conversion in prison, a story of transformation much like Charles', and her request to be baptized privately.

I contacted Chaplain Ray, who visits most of the

prisons, and he confirmed that she too had been born again, completely changed. Listen to this little excerpt from her letter to me: "Grace and peace to you both, from the Father and the Lord Jesus Christ. I'm writing to encourage you concerning your daughter in her illness. I want you both to know I'm praying for her often. Our Lord will meet her need."

Are you suspicious? Does all this sound impossible?

Well, from a purely human standpoint, it might be. I really can't credit the penal system, because at last report, old Charlie Manson is still one mixed-up dangerous dude.

But Susan and Charles Watson are different, changed from the inside out, through a supernatural process the Bible calls being "born again."

And that's good news!

"Therefore if any man is in Christ, he is a new creature, the old things are passed away; behold, new things have come." II Corinthians 5:17

— PAT BOONE[2]

After learning more about Tex Watson's conversion, I decided to write and witness to Charles Manson. He answered with a letter that began, "Here ya go preacher." He told me if I wanted to save something, to save the trees. Here is his handwritten letter.

AGRE Ya
go
preacher P5 page 1   60

Everyone got a big thrill when
they took all my rights in 1969/70
what they didnt realize is that
it was there rights also — the
public servents turned to feed
on the public — The law broke
the law & turned in to the out
law — SIN has more levels than
your personal — God can forgive you
all day but the Sins you have done
as a country still keep rolling — when
the Caps take your children & sell them
& robb you & locked you up & youll see
your sins an me as a person will
reflect back from th. J.D.C. or. when
Boat people & Cubans git jobs as Caps
& work up with th. black & they will do
JUST LIKE your systems
have taught them to do — I seen
a white top Cap & I ask him

Death Row Redemption

is there anything ② I can do to get
you to obay the laws — he said no
I said will you pleas do right he
said no — the next guy for his
job is playing fool under him — a
black cop. The white one will retire
soon & he has taught the black
cop will & he will mindlessy
do for money a job that obays no laws.
The Ghost of that mans sins will
reflect long after his gone. Then there
is sins in many where they bought & sad
rivers & later to mud & waist dumps
forgiveness all day want clean it up &
soon A 2 4 your sins against AT W
will be eye an the hole world — I ask an
Omwean Indian why he believe in Clrist so
much he said all his tryb went to heaven
& they control forever & all the Christans
that put them on the cross will go through
them as they cant git in to heaven — so
as the wheel of life rolls your heaven is in a
dream with all the Indians & others you ve
sin against — the Germans Mexcans Indunx
will be there & there will be no trees

Cult Leader: Charles Manson

ps preach

③

no wild life – Rockefella will be there
with is picture of trees but what
Ever your past made for you in your
past bibles + Children wars will be
there – my heaven will be on earth
because I'm reborn on the earth after
22 years of prison – all have their
water clear + air clean + wild life
only I'll be alone + I understand sin
better than you may think – you think
in a thought pattern when your
reborn the old thought patterns are
Complectly gone – That would be
Crazey to you + you would die.
I've got one world + one in my Earth –
+ I've been cleaning up ATWA with
Every that I Can – I would give them
Rock + Roll music all the way to the
grave yard + Let them have drugs
+ sex all the way out to what
ever dream they wanted – What would
be left over would be TREES – Clean
air + water, wild life + the Richous
who came from the graves of
thought – all that gave there lives
to + for Christ would have a

place on Earth at peace for ever & ever – with out people preaching sin & evil with fear + guilt at the same time locking life up in Cages + saying dont Kill with there mouths full of flesh + bloody meet – preachs say dont Kill – Then they go on with they own words to say oh well that dont mean birds or fish or Cows or Croaks or on + on – you mean dont Kill me but you Kill trees + Everything you touch – what you say is not what you have done all that is payment s comeing are your spiritual Bank rupsd + as your Kingdom comes to its End my Kingdom comes to its begaing – my rebirth is moneing will + my dreams on earth are the Real cross far love NOT the many one one day oll take ALL crosss down –

He made no public statement about ever receiving Christ.

Chapter 17

DRUG CARTEL HIT MAN:
JESSE RAMIREZ

I WAS INVITED TO preach at one of the toughest prisons in America, the federal maximum-security penitentiary in Allenwood, Pennsylvania. I recall talking to the officer escorting me from the lobby to the main prison entrance. He asked me to lay my hand flat so he could take an imprint of my palm. I wasn't sure why he was doing that. I asked about it, and the officer explained that the main entrance gate would not open until it read the imprint of my hand.

I said, "That's pretty cool technology."

He sort of sneered and said, "Man, some of these guys would cut your hand off and come out with your hand. This is a high-max penitentiary!"

It was in this prison that I met a Colombian drug cartel hit man, Jesse Ramirez. Here is Jesse's story.

> I was born in Colombia, the oldest of five brothers. Our father had us studying in a private school. My dream was to someday become a surgeon. We each had our own room, and our family was happy. We were not envious of others but happy for their family happiness as well. But the winds of tragedy interrupted my mother's life. My dreams were destroyed like the mighty waves of the ocean crash down the castle of sand on the beach. My father fell in love with another woman, and he left our family. He abandoned us, [leaving] my mother when I was eight years old.

MISTREATED BY FAMILY

> My mother sold everything we had, and we moved to a rented room, all six of us. She began to wash and iron clothes in the homes of the rich. Her mother started a small business of making and selling pies to help support us. She asked me and my brother Wilson to sell

pies so we could help with our family expenses. Some of my uncles were jealous because our grandmother was helping us. They mistreated us and would tell us we were the reason our grandmother had to work, and they began to verbally and physically abuse us. I had never known anything like this until I began associating with thieves, prostitutes, homosexuals, and drug pushers. They were like our family and had been abandoned by their parents.

I began to rob at every opportunity available. My mother tried to change me, and she began to punish me. She was brutal, releasing all of her frustration on me. Once she hung me by my feet with a cord and lit some newspapers to burn my arms and legs. At another time, she tried to strangle me with the stick of a broom by placing it around my throat till one of our friends tore down the door of the room. I was subject to my mother, who was about six feet tall and weighed 180 pounds. On another occasion, she tied my hands behind my shoulders and she would stick my head in a tank of water. Another time she took me to the kitchen underneath the pots where the grill was where she cooked. She took my hands, and she placed them in the broiler of the grill.

I cannot tell you how I felt in those moments, but I hated my mother! Yet, at the same time, I loved her. My hatred controlled me, the way I hated my parents for all that happened to us. I did not see love nor compassion anywhere. That was all I wanted!

Fame in the World of Crime

I tried to find work. But I began working at robbing again, and right away I was caught. For the first time, I went to jail. I was there for seven months, and it was there I met some other bank robbers. They told me when I got out I could meet up with them in Medellin. I did, and things got worse.

I would go in and out of prison. Drugs, alcohol, women, and money consumed my life, and I felt all powerful. I no longer tolerated anything from anybody, not one insult, a bad look or a stare, nothing of that fashion. I became very daring. I did not care about anything. Every time we were going to do something bad, I wanted to be first, and for this reason I gained fame in the world of crime. They called me Crazy Jesse, and many wanted me to work with them.

Within a short time, we were ordered to kill a very powerful man in the world of drugs. He had gotten involved with our bosses and had to pay—with his life. That is how I became connected with assassins for pay. I did not care anything about killing. It was like killing a chicken. No one felt any compassion for me. How is it now that I should have feelings? This is how I would get back at the world that hated me. And I hated it! The hatred was like acid eating me.

Those in the Medellin cartel showed me many things—how to kidnap, how to murder, and all types of evil in the war against other families from the cartels of Medellin and Cali.

I began to depend on witchcraft. I wanted Satan to make a pact with me. I called on him, and I told him I would sell my soul if he would give me what I asked for....I attended a black mass, where they demonstrated and told me things I did not understand. I was very emotional. I only cared about power. I thought I was powerful. The lie of Satan made me feel invincible.

The time came when I traveled to the United States of America, the promised land, I had been told. They said we would have millions of dollars.

I met a lady in New York, and she commented about a

Drug Cartel Hit Man: Jesse Ramirez

man who owed her about $500,000 but refused to pay it. She asked my help to recuperate this money.

Shortly afterwards, with her two brothers, the four of us kidnapped this man's son. We told the man to pay, and we would not cause him harm. We warned him not to inform the police or we would kill his son. Everything was agreed upon, but the ransom didn't happen because the man wasn't able to get to the agreed-upon location.

Having failed, we killed the kidnapped person. Two months later we were arrested in Los Angeles. We were transferred to Miami, and our trial began. One of the brothers turned state's witness so that he would not receive the death sentence.

I was used to being in prison. My dependence on alcohol and drugs was so great that I felt I had to escape. They would kill me, or I would succeed.

One Sunday morning, I heard a preacher named Jimmy Swaggart speak of something that caught my attention. He spoke of the love of Jesus Christ, and for some reason I could not move. It seemed as though he could see me. He knew my need and my problem. Something very strange surrounded me.

Right away I felt two huge hands inside me take my heart. I began to cry and tremble like a wet chicken, and something deep within me said, "I am Jesus, and I love you, and I want to make you a new creature." When the program was over, I ran to find a Bible, and I began to read it, though I could not understand what was happening.

Afterwards a man came to my cell. He was with me for one day. He then asked me if I had received Jesus as my Savior. I answered no, and he asked if I would like to do it. I told him yes, and he had me repeat the sinner's prayer. I received Christ as my Savior that day, and I began to seek Him with all my heart. I had lived in a bad way, but now I would live for my Lord with great faithfulness!

The Bible says that all is possible for whoever believes. I beg you to pray for me so that the Lord will continue to use me and also for my beloved wife, Gloria, who works with the prison ministry. Pray not just that we might be used, but also that we would not be filled with air like the globe and we would not forget the work God has done in us, so that in everything we give our Father all the honor and the glory.

Chapter 18

EXECUTION—JIMMY LEE GRAY

DEATH ROW REDEMPTION

H E TOLD ME of murdering his sixteen-year-old girlfriend
in Arizona. The killing took place many years before the
murder for which he was about to be executed. We had become
somewhat close through the years of correspondence while he
was on death row in Parchman, Mississippi. Jimmy confided in
me. He had served time in Arizona prisons for the murder of
his girlfriend. He had been out of prison only eighteen months
and appeared to be doing well when he committed one of the
most despicable crimes in Mississippi history.

He was convicted of the kidnapping and murder of a
three-year-old girl in Pascagoula, Mississippi. The young child,
Deressa Jean Scales, was suffocated in a mud-filled ditch. There
is no doubt that Jimmy Lee Gray was the most hated man I
have ever met. Prison officials hated him, guards hated him,
other inmates hated him, his own parents forsook him, Jimmy
hated himself, and the State of Mississippi wanted him dead.

It was June 25, 1976, when Jimmy Lee Gray committed one
of the most ignominious murders in the annals of Mississippi
crime. It was about 5:00 p.m. when Deressa Scales' mother
noticed her daughter was missing. After searching for the
little girl, the mother notified police. The police arrived in
response to the phone call, and a search began. Police inqui-
ries revealed that the little girl was friendly with Gray and his
live-in girlfriend.

Police found Gray around midnight at the hamburger stand
where his girlfriend worked. Gray had shoulder-length hair,
was of a slight build, and had thin, sunken facial features. He
was still a young man when the crime took place. The police
explained the situation, and Gray volunteered to help find the
girl. Police patrolman Michael Whitmore said Gray was very
cooperative. When Gray was in the patrol car, he was asked if

182

Execution—Jimmy Lee Gray

he had a record. He readily admitted he was on parole from Arizona for the murder of his girlfriend. It had been only eight years since Gray committed his first murder. Gray had been tried and convicted in Arizona and received a twenty-year sentence for second-degree murder. He served seven years in Arizona prisons and was paroled in 1975.

Police took Gray to headquarters, and he was overtaken by fear. He thought they knew, and he knew he would never get out of there. Even though he had not confessed to the crime, he knew they would find out. Gray said, "If I take you to her, will you help me?"[1]

He led officers to a bridge that spanned Black Creek. The first story he told the officers was that he had stopped his truck short of the bridge, and the little girl was playing along the side when she fell into the water. He told police he thought about diving in to rescue her but was afraid. He also said he ran to the west side of the bridge to see if she had floated under the bridge, but he never saw her again. These were lies.

Marriage was on the horizon, and he had a good job and reasons to be content in life. He had just finished working on his car at the apartments where the little girl also lived. He was going to test-drive his car, and Deressa asked if she could ride with him. In a statement, Gray said that he "got to thinking, that I might be getting into trouble. I might should not have taken Deressa because I might get into some kind of trouble. Anyway, the more I drove, the more worried I got, the more sure I was that I was going to get into trouble."

When asked if he had molested the girl, Gray said, "I really did not do much to her....I did not undress her." He did admit touching her genital area but denied molesting her. He said under oath that the girl fell into a ditch and "sort of coughed....

DEATH ROW REDEMPTION

She was in the water...a lot less than a minute." The investigation revealed the ditch "contained only three inches of water over two inches of soft silt."

The statement revealed that Gray had placed the "wet and muddy" body into the trunk of his car and drove to the bridge, where he threw the girl's body into the water. The statement also indicated he then returned to Pascagoula, where he washed his car and visited a restaurant before returning to his apartment.[2]

Jimmy Lee Gray was convicted of capital murder. He said, "I would gladly accept the death penalty if this would bring the little girl back." Gray wanted to die and felt he should die. A jury sentenced him to death in the Mississippi gas chamber.

"Don, I wish I could help you understand a person like me so perhaps you could help someone else...but, Don, I don't understand myself. Maybe I was crazy. The psychiatrists say I'm not. Do you think I could have been demon possessed? I think I was." Jimmy hesitated only briefly, not even long enough for me to respond.

"I killed my girlfriend for no reason, and I killed this little girl for no reason, absolutely no reason. But I swear I didn't rape that little girl, I swear I didn't....Maybe I was an animal of some kind, but I didn't do that. It don't matter now. They're gonna kill me in a few hours. I just want you to know, it's important to me that you know I did not rape that little girl."

Did I believe him? I guess I did, as there was nothing for him to gain by lying. I asked him about evidence and if he disputed it in court. "No, I didn't, Don. This would help them get a murder conviction. I felt I deserved to die. At the time, I wanted to die. They said they had a small sampling of semen that proved I sexually assaulted her. I knew they didn't because

Execution—Jimmy Lee Gray

I knew I didn't do it. But see, Don, it didn't matter. I wanted to die."

HATED BY EVERYONE

Jimmy tried to commit suicide three times while in the county jail in Pascagoula. "God, how I hated myself! I couldn't accept what I had done to that innocent child and to that family. I was so overwhelmed with guilt and remorse, I hated myself, and I knew everyone else hated me.

"Once I slit my wrist and lay on the floor in a pool of my own blood, wanting to die, trying to die, and couldn't. An officer sat right outside of my cell and watched me, hoping I would die. For some reason I didn't, and after waiting a long period of time, he finally called for help. I wanted to die and couldn't; the little girl wanted to live and couldn't. God, how I hurt!

"You know, I almost welcomed the hate everyone showed toward me because I felt I deserved to be hated. Don, my own mother came to see me in the county jail. She told me, 'Jimmy, if you did what they say you did, I hope they do kill you!' I never saw my mother after that. I guess you could say I was forsaken by my parents. I guess I deserved that too."

When Jimmy's mother was asked to respond to the charge, she said, "I was horrified, I was shocked. I felt so much anger I just wanted to beat him in the face." She felt no responsibility, and she felt no love for him. "He was always a moody boy. He had the tendency to always associate with boys who were on the borderline of being in trouble." Twice he stole motorcycles and ran away from home. Once he stole money from his grandmother's purse. He had minor scrapes with the law prior to the Arizona murder.

His mother said, "I know his life will not bring that baby back, but we have to stop this somewhere. This is the second girl my son has killed in less than ten years. If I had been on that jury, I would have voted the same way they did! I would not want to see my son out on the streets; I would be afraid to. I guess I love him; I'm not really sure."

She also said in response to the Gary Gilmore execution in Utah the day before that perhaps that would clear the way for her son to be executed. She wanted her son in the gas chamber. "I told Jimmy I hoped he found peace in the next world. He certainly hasn't found it here."

Her visit to Jimmy was six days after the body was found. She had come to Pascagoula for his wedding, but instead she found he had murdered again. She claimed she never knew the details of the Arizona killing. "If I had, I would have never pushed Arizona officials for his parole." She said Arizona officials had led her to believe it was more or less an accident. I guess she was not at the trial, and perhaps she did not read the newspaper accounts of the murder. He strangled the girl with his hands and then with his belt. Officers said he used a wire to choke her to death. Had Gray served his full twenty years, he would have still been in prison, and Deressa Scales would have perhaps lived a normal life. Who can speculate how each of their lives may have been different?

"SAYING I WAS SORRY WOULD NOT HELP AT ALL"

Gray said, "I can't tell you what kind of feelings I had. I mean, they are pretty much indescribable. My entire body hurt from the pain of guilt. It was like I was under a dark, dense cloud all the time. No, it was more than being under a dark cloud—I

Execution—Jimmy Lee Gray

was in it. Darkness was thick around me. I kept thinking about those poor parents who would never see their little girl again. I hurt so much for them, and I knew they didn't want to hear from me. Saying I was sorry would not help at all. I knew I could not undo my horrible deed. What terrible pain they must have felt compared to mine."

Jimmy asked if I thought he was crazy. I said, "No, I don't Jimmy—not now anyway. I can't speak for those years I did not know you. Obviously, there was definitely something wrong. What did your psychiatrist and psychologist say?"

"Well, she said I was definitely not crazy. But Don," he said, "I think that's because she wants me executed also. See, there is a law that states a 'lunatic' cannot be executed. I'm sure the state has some influence in her evaluation and assessment of me, but I kind of liked her. Maybe that is her honest opinion."

I asked Jimmy if he could look back on his life and pinpoint where his bizarre thinking began. "Why did the thought of killing ever come to your mind? Do you know? Did it just pop into your mind? Did you plot and plan to kill your girlfriend? What was going on in your life at the time?"

Jimmy told me he remembered well how it all took place and when the thought of killing first came to his mind. "Sure," he said. "Don't you think I've explored that a million times in my mind and heart? Sure I remember."

Jimmy was friends with his girlfriend's brother. The family of the victim, Elda Louise Prince, helped Jimmy to stay in school and befriended him in many ways. The mother of the slain daughter said they would buy Jimmy clothes and take him with them to ball games and to fish. She acknowledged that Jimmy had problems at home but didn't know what they were.

187

Jimmy said, "We lived in this small town in Arizona, the kind of town that was all on one side of the highway and railroad tracks—you know, town on one side, desert on the other. Sometimes, after school, my girlfriend and I would go out into the desert and fool around. We would cross over the highway and the railroad tracks and just walk to some secluded spot and make love. Can you picture a little town like that in Arizona?"

Actually, I could. Jimmy had painted a good picture of the town where he lived. Parker, Arizona, is on the Colorado River and the California state line. The population is around three thousand. It's about forty miles north of I-10.

"Well, Don, I had been reading some magazines—you know, those true detective magazines—that tell all the gruesome details of violent crimes. Well, I had been reading those things for a couple of weeks when one night it was like this feeling just swept over me. I started wondering what it would be like to kill someone. I know that sounds pretty weird, but I couldn't shake that thought. It sort of became a haunting type of thought that was always there." This was when strong demonic thinking crept into his life and eventually began to control Jimmy. This was a good description of how demons enter in and a typical source of their doorways.

"Look, Don, this is pretty far out. I'm only telling you these things to help you understand me and maybe help you to understand someone else somewhere down the line."

I nodded. "I know, Jimmy. I appreciate you sharing it." I assured him that I was interested for those very reasons.

He continued, "After carrying that curious thought in my mind several days and nights, maybe even weeks, I knew I was going to kill someone. And I was such a coward. I even knew it would be my girlfriend."

Execution—Jimmy Lee Gray

MURDER HAD BECOME AN OBSESSION

"I am so ashamed to even talk about this," Jimmy said. "The thing is, Don, is that it's the truth. It was who I was and how I thought. I knew the day I was going to kill her, even as we walked into the desert. I knew that I was going to commit murder, and it was all about me, and I didn't even give a thought to her. I was consumed with evil. It was really like something had come over me. I guess I was demon possessed. How else could I do something like what I did?

"When we got to a place in the desert that we had been before, I could feel the murderous rage rise within me. I had never felt anything like that before. I was such a coward that I could not do it. We had sex, and I began to humiliate her and insult her to make her mad at me. I told her she was a lousy lover and all kinds of things like that until she finally slapped me—she began to give me a reason to fight her. I strangled her to death. I'm so ashamed to say all of that. I was such a sorry person. You know what was really strange about it—when it was over, the feeling left me. The horrid murderous rage was gone. I deserved the twenty-years-to-life sentence I got. They should have never let me out, but at the time I thought I was ready to live in society."

I started going into prisons in Texas the same year Jimmy Lee Gray was released from Arizona. I didn't know him or anything about the crime. The Arizona prison system is like the hundreds of others I have visited. I think I have been in all their state complexes over the years, as well as the federal prisons in the state. I'm not sure which prison Jimmy was released from, but I have been there. I have also been with inmates on death row in Florence, Arizona. Jimmy Lee Gray was not on death row. It seems from knowing about his crime

DEATH ROW REDEMPTION

that he should have been. Seven years for a premeditated, cold-blooded murder really makes no sense.

Jimmy agreed. "I should have been executed for that senseless killing, but I guess I was glad I didn't get a worse sentence. To be honest, Don, I thought I was prepared to go back out into the world."

He continued, "One other time this thing came over me after I had spent seven years in prison. I remember so well. I would have killed again. I had been out of prison for a while, and I was in Chicago. I had not experienced any temptations to kill or even to think like I once thought, and my mind was fairly normal in that area. I recall one evening while walking on a somewhat dim-lighted street that a girl was ahead of me and that feeling came over me. It was the same driving force that caused me to kill my girlfriend. I knew immediately that I was going to kill that girl. I wish I could explain this to help you understand. It all seems so weird, but I knew it was the same thing that drove me to kill before.

"How could this be? I never had any thoughts like that while I was in prison. Actually, this was the first time since the murder. It was the same strong feeling that was driving me, the same demonic force as before. The thought was so heavy in my mind that I couldn't dismiss it. It was the same demonic force, I know. I couldn't control it. I didn't know this girl.

"However, as I got closer to her, someone came around the corner. In that brief moment, the feeling left me. As quickly as it came, it left. I think about that often. I don't know how to explain this, Don. What could it have been besides demons? I didn't know this person, and I to this day don't know why I would have killed her, but I was going to. I was really a messed-up person, but most of me was normal and I functioned well in other areas."

He didn't talk to me much about his childhood except to say he came from a very dysfunctional home. Once he said, "Don, I remember once when I was very small that my dad held me by the feet and dangled me outside of the car from the driver's window. I don't remember how old I was; I had to be pretty young. I could see the highway stripes below me as he sped down the highway, and [he was] telling my mom, 'Jimmy won't cry. Look, Jimmy's tough. He won't cry.' I guess he thought he was making me tough or something. It didn't work. I've never been so scared, and I'm the closest thing to a coward that you will ever meet."

He mentioned to me that he never really felt loved. "Don, I'm sure my parents did love me, but I never felt loved."

Jimmy had accepted Christ while in prison and knew he had been forgiven by God, but he also knew no one in this world would forgive him, and he couldn't forgive himself. As I mentioned, Jimmy Lee Gray was without doubt the most hated man I have ever met. The things he had done were despicable, beyond any human reasoning. They were horrible crimes. Everyone hated Jimmy Lee. But he was easy to talk to, and I had compassion for him.

As was custom, his cell was closest to the gas chamber. He could see it every day. That is by design. While I had written to Jimmy for some time, I had been to see him only a few times and had also preached on death row. The chaplain then, Ron Padgett, was a good man, and he and I had become friends. I had lunch with him and his wife in their home on one of my visits to Parchman.

In 1983 there had not been an execution in the US for nineteen years because of judicial challenges to capital punishment.

The courts granted several stays of execution for Jimmy. I don't recall how many times it was postponed. Jimmy had asked me to be there with him, and I went several times before it actually happened. Jimmy Lee Gray's execution was the first one in Mississippi since the capital punishment had been ruled unconstitutional by the Supreme Court in 1972 in *Furman v. Georgia*, causing states to draft new statutes to address the issues in the ruling.

Parchman, Mississippi, is really just a place where a prison is located. The Mississippi State Penitentiary is a 2,500-bed facility that was built on 18,000 acres in 1901. Before the gas chamber, the state had a portable electric chair that was brought in for executions. The state no longer executes by gas chamber; in 1984 lethal injection became an option for putting condemned inmates to death, and lethal gas was removed as an option in 1998.

As you drive through the prison grounds, you are reminded of prison movies with road chain gangs, outdoor solitary confinement boxes, and prison life in the '40s and '50s. There are many prison camps and buildings on the huge plot of land. One is the death row and execution building. Although the gas chamber is gone and prison conditions have changed, I remember it well.

I drove from my home in Bedford, Texas, to Cleveland, Mississippi, a town about sixteen miles from Parchman. My plan was to spend the day with Jimmy Lee Gray the day before his execution. The execution was to take place at midnight. I don't really know what emotions I expected, but I knew there would be some that I had not experienced before. I prayed, and I received the Holy Spirit's direction the best way I knew how.

The prison was expecting a large corps of media to cover

Execution—Jimmy Lee Gray

the event. A large tent was set up just inside the gate with many microphones and TV cameras. However, on that same day, Korean Airlines flight 007 veered off course and flew into Russian airspace. The Soviets sent two fighter jets to intercept the commercial plane. The fighter pilots tried to make contact with the passenger jet, but there was no response. The Soviets fired a missile at the plane, which then crashed into the Sea of Japan, killing all 269 people on board. That was world-shattering news, and the execution became of little interest.

I had driven the road to Parchman several times, but that day was different. There would be no stay of execution. It was going to happen. I couldn't believe what I was seeing between the small town of Drew and Parchman. State highway patrol cars lined the highway, there to "celebrate" the execution of a convicted child killer.

As I entered the prison gates, it was also different than before. There were officers in full dress on horseback patrolling the prison grounds. It was like a military event, for lack of a better description. I was taken to the death row facility and escorted again to Jimmy's cell. Many of the men on death row knew me from previous visits and from preaching at a death row chapel service. Generally, they would speak, and we would exchange some small talk. Not that day. It was silent—sort of a strange reverence for the one to be executed.

I visited with Jimmy from just outside his cell. We talked through the bars. One of the many events that stands out to me was an officer bringing his twelve-year-old son back to Jimmy's cell. He pointed at Jimmy and told his son, "There he is, son. There's the man who likes to kill babies. But we're gonna get him tonight!"

I didn't know what to say when he left with his son. It was

an awkward moment. Jimmy sensed I was unsettled and said, "That's OK, Don. I've heard it about every day since I've been here."

Not long after that, an officer came from the opposite end of the death row run. He had waist chains with him. He said, "Gray, you've got a phone call." Now, that's something that never happens. You can't just call a death row inmate. Jimmy was shackled and chained and led down the hall in his red jumpsuit. After a few minutes, he was led back. I remember the scene from where I stood to where he took the phone call. It was a wall phone near the entrance to the building. Handcuffed and in waist chains, he held the phone up to his ear. He shuffled back and was locked back in his cell. "That was my dad. Don, I've waited thirty-four years to hear him say, 'I love you.' I guess that doesn't matter. What matters is that I love him." Neither of Jimmy's parents came to the execution.

There was an evil and eerie silence. I don't know if it is possible to describe. Later that evening, we shared a last meal together. Jimmy had requested pizza. Another man who visited Jimmy was with us as well. The chaplain had also arranged for the four of us to observe Communion together. The room we met in was just around the corner from the gas chamber. As we partook in the Lord's Supper, Jimmy asked, "Don, is there anything you want me to tell Jesus for you personally in a few minutes?"

Without hesitating I said, "Yeah, Jimmy, tell Him I love Him!"

He grinned. "You got it."

It was only minutes later that he was strapped into the chair and then died from the gas released into the chamber. The executioner was drunk, and the execution was botched.[3] There

Execution—Jimmy Lee Gray

was an iron post directly behind the chair Jimmy was strapped in, and when the gas did not kill him instantly, he banged his head on the post as he convulsed. It went on for several minutes until they escorted everyone out of the witness box.

I recall the bizarre feeling of getting into my car to leave the prison. I had barely started the engine and was still in front of the death row prison building when I heard on the radio: "Mississippi officials carried out the state's first execution since 1964 when Jimmy Lee Gray was put to death in the gas chamber..."

It was over. I remember driving in the darkness from the prison and by the media tent. The tent was empty. In a strange way I was glad there was no national news coverage. The highway back to Cleveland was now void of state and local police presence. I don't know if I can describe the range of emotions I was experiencing.

Newspapers carried the Associated Press story the next day:

A gold-colored hearse took Mr. Gray's body from the prison to a funeral home at Indianola, about 40 miles away. The body, claimed by a Natchez church group that had befriended Mr. Gray, was buried in an undisclosed plot after an unannounced 7 A.M. service.

Dennis Balske, an Alabama lawyer who Thursday lost an 11th-hour plea for the United States Supreme Court to block the execution, said after watching that Mr. Gray had suffered a "painful death." Mr. Balske's appeals had challenged the gas chamber as cruel and unusual punishment.

Mr. Gray, who in his younger years had a reputation of being a loner with a violent temper, spent his final hours visiting with friends and ministers. His mother, who had twice called on the Mississippi authorities to execute her son, telephoned Mr. Gray hours before his death, officials said. He also talked by telephone with his father and brother, all from outside the state.[4]

Thank God for Jesus. Thank God that He is no respecter of persons, that He came to seek and to save the lost. You see, Jesus was on death row. He ate with publicans and sinners. He was falsely accused and falsely convicted. He forgave an executed man who hung on the cross next to Him. He was acquainted with grief and sorrow.

Perhaps you remember that a notorious inmate was released and Jesus got executed in his stead. Jesus understands the plight of the condemned, the victim, and the state. He shed His blood for all men, and He lives today ready to receive any who will call upon Him as Savior.

I pray there be no more victims, no more criminals, no more injustice. We all know that won't happen in this world, but a day is coming when Jesus Himself will rule and reign in a kingdom that only knows righteousness. I want as many as I can reach to be in that kingdom. I want you there. God wants you there too. That's why He sent Jesus into this world. Jesus did not come into the world to condemn but to set free:

> For God did not send His Son into the world to condemn the world, but that the world through Him might be saved. He who believes in Him is not condemned; but he who does not believe is condemned already, because he has not believed in the name of the only begotten Son of God.
>
> —John 3:17–18

We don't have to do anything to be under the sentence of condemnation; our sin nature is condemnation enough. We must act to be freed from that condemnation. Salvation is a

Execution—Jimmy Lee Gray

conscious act on our part to receive what Jesus has already done for us. That's what Jimmy did; he just received the redemption God offers to all through His Son, Jesus Christ. And while still under the condemnation of the state, Jimmy was freed from the law of sin and death by Jesus. Thank God for Jesus!

Here ya go preacher

Don Dickerman
Box 575
Hurst, Texas 76053

NORTH BAY, CA 949
PM
1 A
23 JUN
1988

Chapter 19

EXECUTION—FOREIGN JURISDICTION

A S HORRIBLE AS the executions I witnessed were, another one was worse. I'll share what I can about it, although I wasn't there. It was in a foreign jurisdiction, but it was the most publicized of all executions—and people still talk about it.

Police officers sold T-shirts that read "Raulerson, make my day!" when J. D. Raulerson was executed for killing a police officer. At this other execution, state police stripped the very clothes off the man's back and then, in full view of the crowd, gambled for them.

At the execution of Jimmy Lee Gray in Mississippi, a few people gathered to protest his execution, but they caused no problems. A few people also gathered at Raulerson's execution to protest the death penalty. However, at the foreign jurisdiction, no one protested the execution; instead, a mob gathered to ensure there would be one.

It was a morning in springtime when people gathered at the execution site. Some sat down and watched as if it were an entertainment event. Others stood and jeered. Some just passed by on their way to somewhere else, but as they passed, they paused long enough to yell insults at the one being executed.

THE RELIGIOUS CROWD

I recall how the mother of J. D. Raulerson reacted when she was led away from her soon-to-be-executed son. She screamed in horror. She was out of control. She held her fist in anger toward the heavens as she wept. When Jimmy Lee Gray was executed, his mother was not there. She had told him in the county jail that if he had done what he was charged with, she hoped they did kill him.

At this other execution, the mother of the man being executed was present. She stood directly in front of her son and

Execution—Foreign Jurisdiction

wept silent tears. I have been directly in front of someone being executed; it is not easy. I can't imagine a mother being in that position. She never spoke; quivering lips and painful tears choked away any words she may have wanted to say. Some friends stood with her to console and comfort. A personal friend of her son, perhaps his closest friend, was also there. As death began to replace life, he spoke to his mother and his friend. He asked his friend to look after his mother as though he were her son. They both nodded in agreement, as their brokenness would not allow words to come.

J. D. Raulerson, in his last words, offered forgiveness to the prison superintendent for taking his life. Most did not believe he really meant that but was only trying to embarrass the state. Similar words of forgiveness were spoken at this other execution. This man, however, prayed to God to forgive the people, stating that they really didn't understand what they were doing. What puzzles me is how the religious crowd could be so bloodthirsty. If anyone should be willing to show compassion and mercy, it's the religious folks. Instead, they were actually behind it all. Even today it is the "religious" crowd who often cry loudest for the death of criminals.

The two executions I witnessed left an indelible impression on my life. Certainly, I will never forget them. However, this other execution and the events that surrounded it changed my life forever. When the alleged criminal came out of the courtroom and jail area, it was plain to see that he had been beaten. He was bleeding, his back torn to shreds by a whip, and he looked so tired and weak. He had been humiliated the entire night. His eyes scanned the crowd as though looking for a friendly face. The trial, if you can call it that, had been a ridiculous mockery of justice. His closest friends had forsaken him.

Loneliness showed in his face. The police pointed him toward the execution area. This one would take place outside, accommodating the mob who wanted to witness the man's death.

It was a pretty good distance to walk from the courtroom to the execution site. And as he walked, there were some ugly scenes. People spat on him and called him names. They slapped him and pushed him. They pulled on his hair and beard.

The man was in his early thirties with most of his life still ahead of him, just like J. D. Raulerson and Jimmy Lee Gray. And just like Raulerson and Gray, this man looked normal. A frequent comment I hear from people who go into prison for the first time is their surprise that the inmates look normal. People often have preconceived ideas that convicts sport shaved heads, have scars on their faces, and wear black and white striped uniforms. No, they usually look like the guy next door.

There were no distinctive features about this man. He was a pretty average-looking guy. He was born in a village in the suburbs. His mother was from a religious family. Like many today who wind up on death row, he was born in obscurity. He was not even born in what would be his hometown. His parents were traveling, so he was born in a strange town and a strange place.

Many times inmates take me back to their younger days in an effort to find a cause for the events that led to their conviction. This man's infancy was out of the ordinary. His parents had to leave the country because of death threats against him before he was even two years old. He lived in a foreign country until it was safe to return. His home was filled with the tension of impending threats on his life. He was raised in what we might call poverty-level conditions, even after his family returned from the foreign country to the small town he would call home.

HE WAS ACQUAINTED WITH GRIEF

I was able to locate very little information on this man's youth. Perhaps it was uneventful. I do know he worked as a carpenter's helper. He attended Hebrew school and was familiar with Jewish religion and the Hebrew Scriptures.

A noticeable change took place in this man's life about the age of twelve. He wandered away from his family on a trip to the city. He was doing his own thing and was not really concerned that he had been separated from his family. When his mother found him, she scolded him for the behavior. His explanation was that he was doing business for his father. It was this attitude that would one day get him executed.

As an adult, he learned to live with death threats and actual attempts on his life. He was a man who knew sorrow and grief as constant acquaintances. Some found him despicable. Virtually all inmates can tell you about dealing with the pain of rejection. If anyone ever knew rejection, it was this man. He was both popular and unpopular. He was loved and hated. Some heaped praise upon him, while others sought to kill him. He was gentle yet perceived by some as threatening. He managed to slip through the crowd on one occasion when the people were incensed by his speech and intended to kill him. Several times he tried to tell his closest friends that death was coming, but they never really understood.

The men who were his closest associates were so impressed with him that they quit their jobs to be a part of what he did. These were men he personally sought out. They gave up everything without hesitation or reconsideration to participate in what he was doing. These men so believed in what he was doing that they willingly lived without any of life's luxuries. They did not understand that their lives were also going to be in danger when they consented to join him, because death was stalking him.

THE LAST MEAL

I shared Jimmy Lee Gray's last meal, along with a few others of his friends. He asked me and some of the others what we liked to eat; the consensus was pizza and tacos, and that is what we ate before we had a small Communion service. I was there with J. D. Raulerson in Florida when his last meal was brought to his cell. He turned it down, and the officer stationed at the front of his cell ended up eating it. However, the last meal for this other man was not served by the state. He called his friends together for what he knew would be his last meal.

He had to borrow someone's home for his last meal. He was homeless, although not in the context we now use that word. He turned down an opportunity to be very wealthy; he was essentially offered the world, but he refused it. Sometimes poverty is a choice.

It was the season of the Jewish Passover, and he observed this special time with his closest friends. It was at his last meal that he told them the state was going to kill him. What a somber moment that must have been. He told his friends tough times were ahead. The police would be coming soon. One of his friends vowed that the police would have to kill him first.

Before Jimmy Lee Gray's execution, Chaplain Ron Padgett asked that we sing a hymn. We all joined hands and sang a familiar hymn, even though our hearts were heavy with the burden of the one to be executed. Before this foreign execution, the little band of men also sang a hymn before they adjourned from that last meal. Then they went to a place like a city park with a garden, and he asked three of his closest friends to go with him to a place of solitude. He wanted them with him because he knew it was just a matter of time before he would be captured. They were all tired from a long day and the emotion of the moment. He could sense they didn't really understand. He asked them to pray for him as he left to go further into the garden to pray alone. When he returned, they were asleep. He knew he was going to have to bear the agony alone.

THE SNITCH AND THE FALSE WITNESSES

As the man spoke to his sleeping friends to wake them up, a lynch mob of police officers and religious leaders arrived. They were angry and bloodthirsty. One of his so-called friends had snitched on him. After the so-called friend pointed him out, the police took him into custody.

As they were leading him away, his friend who boasted he would die for him slashed at one member of the mob and cut off his ear. I'm sure there was a gasp from the crowd as they sensed a violent confrontation was about to happen. You don't assault someone during an arrest and it go unnoticed. However, the accused calmly told his friend to allow it all to happen and then reached out and healed the man's ear.

It puzzles me that this incident went almost unnoticed. What man can replace a severed part of the human body without sutures, disinfectant, adhesive, or other medical supplies? The wounded man touched his ear to assure it was in place and working. He stood stunned and amazed. Yet the amazing deed went virtually unnoticed in the blind rage of the people who wanted to see the man in custody killed. Although he was in custody, he was the one who seemed to be in control.

The police did not load the man in a squad car and drive off. Instead, they walked him through the city streets as a spectacle for the people to mock and jeer. It was indeed a time of darkness, and it lasted all night. The man's friends were caught up with fear and uncertainty. Most of them lost themselves in the mob or fled for their own safety, although one friend lingered and followed at a distance.

The man in custody was taken before an assembly of political and religious leaders at the courthouse. The next few hours were some of the most difficult hours a man could imagine.

No one had informed this man of his rights. He had no rights. When he was arrested, no one said, "You have the right to remain silent," or "You have the right to an attorney." He had no legal counsel. He was alone and at the mercy of a hostile and corrupt legal system.

They called false witnesses to try to get testimony that would mean the death penalty, but initially were unsuccessful. There was no evidence. Then finally the state found two false witnesses who lied enough to satisfy a corrupt assembly. The man was charged and declared deserving of death based on the testimony of false witnesses.

Court bailiffs blindfolded him. He was slapped in the face and then asked to tell who it was that hit him. His teeth were knocked loose. His face was bloody and marred. His appearance was severely altered from the beating. And that was just the pretrial hearing.

What About His Friends?

No one really knows where most of the accused's friends were while the mob was buzzing with excitement outside the hearing. Friends who had faithfully walked with him all over the countryside for three years, going through tough times and good times together, were nowhere to be found. Perhaps they were disillusioned by the whole thing. Perhaps they thought their dream was over. Whatever the reason, they were not present.

There was one friend, however, who was trying to keep up with the events and yet not be recognized. He was confronted by a girl who accused him of being an associate of the accused. The friend said, "I don't know what you are talking about."

After this denial, he slipped into the porch area. No doubt he could hear the sounds of the beating taking place inside the chamber. Out on the porch another young lady spotted the friend and said, "This fellow was with him."

Again, the friend denied that he was an associate and said, "I do not know the man."

As the friend stood in the shadows, warming himself by the fire of his enemies and trying to be inconspicuous, several others looked at him more closely. They said, "Surely you are one of them; your speech sounds just like his."

This was too much, and the friend cursed and swore and vehemently denied that he knew him. A strange thing happened at that very moment. The sun was beginning to break through the darkness of the night, and in the distance a rooster crowed. The friend who so strongly denied knowing the defendant slipped out of the crowd and disappeared into the early morning cold.

He was trembling, and his lip quivered as he fought tears. For as he heard the rooster crow, he turned and caught the eye of the one to be executed, the one he had just denied. The look was not of anger or disappointment but rather of love and forgiveness.

In the meantime, the accused's so-called friend who had snitched and betrayed him was having a tough time dealing with his conscience. He had taken a bribe to turn the suspect over to the authorities. The bribe money didn't mean as much as he originally thought it might. He went to the authorities and brought back the money. He insisted that his friend was innocent and that he was sorry for what he had done. They only offered a smirk and said, "That's your problem." He threw the money at their feet and left.

Never had he felt so empty. His stomach burned from the agony of knowing he had betrayed his friend. He could not sleep. He couldn't get any peace, and he paced the floor all night. He had no one to turn to with his problem. He was miserable because he could not undo what he had done. It was too late. He couldn't live with what he had done, so he hanged himself.

The authorities didn't know what to do with the returned money since it was blood money. They decided to purchase land that could be used to bury strangers and those who died indigent. It is possible that the betrayer himself may have been the first to be buried in that infamous piece of ground.

THE TRIAL

As the day was breaking, the steps necessary to execute the accused continued. The man was taken from the cellblock area, secured in chains, and delivered to the governor. The governor had the power to issue a death warrant, to grant a stay of execution, or to grant clemency and set the prisoner free.

Execution—Foreign Jurisdiction

As the prisoner stood before the governor in all his innocence, blood dripped from his swollen face. His hands were cuffed behind his back. He refused to reply to the charges against him. The governor was greatly intrigued at his silence. The man's refusal to speak also disturbed the governor because it was obvious he was innocent. Why didn't he speak up? Why didn't he defend himself?

The governor had mixed feelings about the situation. Although he felt certain the man was innocent, he also felt somewhat intimidated by his presence. His wife felt some of the tension also and sent him a note warning him to do the right thing. It was more than just women's intuition; she had actually dreamed that the accused man was innocent. Political pressure, religious leaders clamoring, and the governor's own feelings were making this a difficult decision. Yet the governor thought he had found a way out of his dilemma.

There was a law on the books that permitted the release of a prisoner during Passover. The governor decided to let the people decide which inmate would be released. The governor let them choose between the most notorious prisoner in the jail, a man everyone knew to be guilty of heinous crimes, and the accused who had just been brought before the governor. The governor felt certain this would get him off the hook since the accused man was innocent.

The governor called the people together and made the offer of one of the two prisoners to be released. "Take your pick: this man, who has done nothing, or this man that our court systems have found guilty of many crimes and whom you know to be a criminal." He was sure their consciences would make the right choice obvious. But they chose to release the convicted criminal who deserved punishment. Incredible!

The governor was stunned. "What will I do with this man who is innocent?"

They all cried, "Execute him! Kill him!"

"Why? What has he done wrong?" The governor never got an answer to those last two questions, not from the people and not from the man he was forced to condemn.

Police officers came for the innocent man and beat him across the back with a whip of multiple leather strips with sharp objects in the ends to rip and tear the flesh. Thirty-nine times this whip lashed across the man's back until the flesh was torn to shreds and bleeding. More police officers came, and they removed the man's clothes and put a robe on him. The blood was barely visible as it mingled with the scarlet color of the robe.

The executions I have witnessed had a limited number of witnesses. Most states have strict rules about who can be present when the actual execution takes place—sometimes a few friends or family of the one being executed, a few from the press, and maybe even a few from the victim's family. A limited number of people are allowed to attend a given execution. However, the execution of the innocent man was open to all. People lined the roadway leading from the jail and judgment hall to the execution site on the outskirts of town.

It Is Finished

The executions I witnessed in the gas chamber and the electric chair were very brief, just a matter of seconds before death came. Of the two methods, I would say the gas chamber is most brutal. The foreign execution of the innocent man, however, lasted for hours. Death came agonizingly slow, with

Execution—Foreign Jurisdiction

excruciating pain. The execution was at midday. Just as the execution procedure began, some odd and inexplicable events happened.

A strange silence accompanied ominous-looking clouds. The sky grew very dark. Cloud cover made it seem like nighttime for three full hours. It was kind of like when a storm approaches and you can tell the barometric pressure is dropping. It was eerie. People huddled in little groups, looking at the sky and whispering their thoughts about what was happening.

When the execution started, it was not a pretty sight. Some people got up and left, as the pain of the moment was too much.

I think about this execution often. It changed my life forever. It makes me think of the old spiritual "Were You There?"

> Were you there when they crucified my Lord?
> Were you there when they crucified my Lord?
> O sometimes it causes me to tremble! tremble!
>> tremble!
> Were you there when they crucified my Lord?[1]

You knew as you read through this chapter whose execution I was describing. The man's name was Jesus.

There were two thieves on the crosses next to Him. One cursed Him and challenged His deity; he only wanted out of his situation. The other one seemed to have a remarkable theology. I don't know why—maybe he had been exposed to truth at home, or maybe he even attended Bible school at some point in his life. Regardless, he had biblical doctrine. He confessed that he was a sinner, and he acknowledged Jesus as God. He asked Jesus to save him. He called on the name of the Lord. He also knew there was life after death and that

Jesus was King. Kings have kingdoms. He feared God, which is the beginning of wisdom. The theology of this thief is all the knowledge about God that we need to be saved! Jesus promised the condemned thief that he would be with Him in paradise that same day.

When Jesus spoke from the cross, "It is finished," as the last drop of blood fell to the earth, the ground started moving. It was an earthquake, and it did some damage. Some places were hit harder than others. In some areas large boulders were cracked to pieces, although no loss of life was reported.

In fact, some people actually gained life! People will scoff at this, but it happened. I don't know how it happened; I just know it happened. I don't understand why Hollywood hasn't made a movie about this. Some graves were opened up by the tremor, and bodies of people who had been buried for months and even years came to life. The people got up out of their graves and walked back into town. They went back to relatives and friends, and no one could deny it. Many people witnessed it.

The earthquake also touched a place of worship. Inside the Jewish temple in Jerusalem, a large, thick, heavy curtain separated the holy place from the holy of holies. The curtain, also known as a veil, symbolized the separation between common man and the presence of a holy God. Only the high priest went behind the curtain—and only once a year—to intercede with God for sinful man. When the earth quaked, the curtain was ripped from top to bottom. The manner in which this large curtain was ripped, from heaven downward, was as if by design, by the divine hand of God. Other temple objects were not damaged.

When that curtain was mysteriously ripped in two, God was

Execution—Foreign Jurisdiction

inviting all men to come to Him. There was no more need for an earthly high priest. When Jesus said, "It is finished," it was finished. He did it. He paid the full price for a fallen creation. He accomplished what He came to do.

GIVE ME THE KEYS

I recall how some police made news headlines by cheering as the hearse with the body of J. D. Raulerson drove away. In their disdain and hatred for the killer, they applauded as the body was hauled away. But after Jesus died on the cross, only loving hands touched His body.

Those hands ever so gently lifted the cross from the hole in the ground and carefully laid it down. Tenderly, they pulled the crown of thorns from His head. Tears supplied enough moisture to wipe the blood from His torn flesh. Those loving hands pulled the nails from His hands and feet. Jesus' body was wrapped in linen graveclothes, and spices were applied in a customary manner. His friends placed His body in a borrowed grave.

A borrowed grave? How can you borrow a grave? What is borrowed must be returned. If you are only going to be in a grave for three days, I guess you can borrow one.

As Jesus' loved ones were carrying His body to the tomb, government authorities discussed the possibility of future problems. What if His followers stole His body and claimed Jesus had risen from the dead as He said He would? They decided to station guards outside the tomb and place a government seal across the stone to ensure it would not happen. The body was placed in the tomb, and a stone was rolled up against the entrance. Government officials put a seal across it, and the guards took their places.

DEATH ROW REDEMPTION

Meanwhile the Spirit of God in Jesus had descended into the heart of the earth to set captivity free. The souls of all believers were removed and taken to paradise; one of those souls was the thief who just hours before had called upon Jesus to be his Savior. Just as Jesus had promised, they were together in paradise the same day.

Then Jesus descended into the very heart of evil and confronted Satan. I have a pretty good mental picture of it. Satan obviously comes into the presence of God, as mentioned in the Book of Job. But this time Jesus stepped into Satan's domain. I can see Jesus with His nail-scarred hands extended and a smile on His face saying something like, "I came for the keys. Give Me the keys. I am He that was dead and am alive forevermore, and I will hold the keys of death and hell. Sin will have no more dominion, the grave will lose its victory, and death will lose its sting." As Jesus walked from the presence of a scowling Satan, He raised His arm victoriously and held the keys up to a cheering host of angels. "I have the keys of death, hell, and the grave!"

His body was in the grave for three days, just as Jonah was in the belly of the big fish. The stone did not move for three days. The government felt certain it was over. They had already dismissed thoughts of hearing any more from this impostor. His disciples and friends were dealing with their grief and had perhaps accepted that it was over; maybe Jesus wasn't what He claimed to be. But life conquered death early that Sunday morning.

He who is the life giver rose from the grave, the stone was rolled away, angels folded His graveclothes, and He walked and talked with Mary Magdalene in the garden by the tomb. What a day that must have been.

Execution—Foreign Jurisdiction

Jesus' resurrection is an undeniable part of history. He was seen by the disciples and His close friends, and then He was seen by over five hundred people in Jerusalem.

All that would have been necessary for the story of Jesus' death and resurrection to disappear into history was for one—just one—of the disciples to say it was a lie. Yet they all died saying, "He lives!" They were threatened and tortured to get them to deny the truth, but they would not. They were banished to isolation, shot to death by arrows, beheaded, and crucified upside down, but they claimed to their last breath, "He lives!" I challenge you to find eleven men who will suffer torture, ridicule, stoning, rejection of every sort, threats, brutality, and death for a lie. The disciples, without hesitation, without any question, died for what they knew to be true: He lives!

The thing that really sets apart this execution from all others is the obvious. The One executed was the Son of God. He was totally innocent. He was the spotless, sinless, unblemished Lamb of God slain for the remission of sin. You can't put Him in the same category with anyone, not even with religious leaders.

Jesus is not a religious leader. He is the Son of God. Don't put Him on the same page with Confucius or Muhammad; they were mere mortals, human beings, sinners who died and are still dead. Jesus is alive! The most awesome truth you would discover if you could absorb every book ever written, if you could retain all truth from history, is He lives! And because He lives, you can be redeemed. Because He lives, I can be redeemed. Because He lives, every man and woman on the face of the earth—no matter what they have done—can be redeemed when they choose to accept Jesus as their Savior:

DEATH ROW REDEMPTION

If you confess with your mouth the Lord Jesus and believe in your heart that God has raised Him from the dead, you will be saved.

—ROMANS 10:9

In Him we have redemption through His blood, the forgiveness of sins, according to the riches of His grace.

—EPHESIANS 1:7

A NOTE FROM THE AUTHOR

GOD LOVES YOU deeply. His Word is filled with promises that reveal His desire to bring healing, hope, and abundant life to every area of your being—body, mind, and spirit. More than anything, He wants a personal relationship with you through His Son, Jesus Christ.

If you've never invited Jesus into your life, you can do so right now. It's not about religion—it's about a relationship with the One who knows you completely and loves you unconditionally. If you're ready to take that step, simply pray this prayer with a sincere heart:

Lord Jesus, I want to know You as my Savior and Lord. I confess and believe that You are the Son of God and that You died for my sins. I believe You rose from the dead and are alive today. Please forgive me for my sins. I invite You into my heart and my life. Make me new. Help me to walk with You, grow in Your love, and live for You every day. In Jesus' name, amen.

If you just prayed that prayer, you've made the most important decision of your life. All of heaven rejoices with you, and so do I! You are now a child of God, and your journey with Him has just begun. Please contact my publisher at pray4me@ charismamedia.com so that we can send you some materials that will help you become established in your relationship with the Lord. We look forward to hearing from you.

NOTES

CHAPTER 1

1. David Bulit, "Park View Inn," Abandoned FL, accessed February 11, 2025, https://abandonedfl.com/park-view-inn/.
2. Michael Lambrix, "My First Day on Death Row," Doing Life on Death Row, April 26, 2009, https://doinglifeondeathrow.blogspot.com/2009.
3. Michael Lambrix, "The Christmas Card," Doing Life on Death Row, 2012, https://deathrowjournals.blogspot.com/2018/12/the-christmas-card.html.
4. UPI, "One Killer Reprieved; Another Faces Death," *New York Times*, January 30, 1985, https://www.nytimes.com/1985/01/30/us/around-the-nation-one-killer-reprieved-another-faces-death.html.
5. Ron McAndrew, "Former Florida Warden Haunted by Botched Execution," The Journey of Hope, May 26, 2010, https://thejourneyofhope.blogspot.com/2010_05_01_archive.html.
6. UPI, "Raulerson Executed; Policemen Cheer, Protestors Mourn," *Florida Flambeau*, January 31, 1985, https://archive.org/stream/Florida_Flambeau_1985_Jan/Florida_Flambeau_1985_Jan_djvu.txt.

CHAPTER 3

1. D. Pedersen et al., "Inside America's Toughest Prison," *Newsweek*, October 6, 1986, 46–61.
2. "Cruel and Unusual Punishment: Ruiz," The Texas Politics Project, accessed March 7, 2025, https://texaspolitics.utexas.edu/archive/html/just/features/0505_01/ruiz.html.

CHAPTER 4

1. Ian MacAlpine, "Man Once Called 'Meanest Guy in Prison,'" Whig Standard, December 9, 2012, https://www.thewhig.com/2012/12/09/man-once-called-meanest-guy-in-prison.
2. Jim Cavanagh, *Captured: To Run No More* (CreateSpace, 2012).
3. "I Didn't Have to Try to Escape Anymore: Jim | Canada," Prison Fellowship International, accessed March 7, 2025, https://pfi.org/resources/stories-of-hope/jims-story/.

CHAPTER 6

1. "Betty Lou Beets," Crime Museum, accessed March 20, 2025, https://www.crimemuseum.org/crime-library/famous-murders/betty-lou-beets/; Wikipedia, "Betty Lou Beets," last edited September 22, 2024, https://en.wikipedia.org/wiki/Betty_Lou_Beets; *Beets v. State*," Court of Criminal Appeals of Texas, November 12, 1987, https://law.justia.com/cases/texas/court-of-criminal-appeals/1988/69583-4.html.

CHAPTER 7

1. Jordan Smith, "Without Evidence: Executing Frances Newton," *Austin Chronicle*, September 9, 2005, https://www.austinchronicle.com/news/2005-09-09/288994/.
2. Smith, "Without Evidence."
3. Smith, "Without Evidence."
4. "Pamela Lynn Perillo," Murderpedia, accessed March 8, 2025, https://www.murderpedia.org/female.P/p/perillo-pamela.htm; "Pamela Lynn Perillo, Petitioner-Appellant, v. Gary L. Johnson, Director, Texas Department of Criminal Justice, Institutional Division, Respondent-Appellee, 79 F.3d 441 (5th Cir. 1996)," March 21, 1996, https://law.justia.com/cases/federal/appellate-courts/F3/79/441/556024/; "*Perillo v. Johnson* (2000)," https://caselaw.findlaw.com/court/us-5th-circuit/1438762.html.
5. "'20 Years on Death (Life) Row' The Pam Perillo Story," *Background Check* (podcast), January 31, 2022, https://www.forgivenfelons.org/backgroundcheck/20-years-on-death-life-row-the-pam-perillo-tise-story.
6. "On Death Row, Pickax Murderer Finds a 'New Life,'" *Houston Chronicle*, March 28, 1986.
7. "On Death Row," *Houston Chronicle*.
8. Emily D. Buehler and Rich Kluckow, "Correctional Populations in the United States, 2022—Statistical Tables," Bureau of Justice Statistics, May 2024, https://bjs.ojp.gov/library/publications/correctional-populations-united-states-2022-statistical-tables.
9. Wendy Sawyer, "BJS Report: Drug Abuse and Addiction at the Root of 21% of Crimes," Prison Policy Initiative, June 28, 2017, https://www.prisonpolicy.org/blog/2017/06/28/drugs/.
10. "On Death Row," *Houston Chronicle*.

11. "On Death Row," *Houston Chronicle*.
12. Karla Faye Tucker, "Let Me Open Your Eyes," The Choice Is Yours Program, accessed March 8, 2025, https://www.the-choice-is-yours.com/karlafayetucker.html.

CHAPTER 9

1. Mark Driscoll, "Porn-Again Christian," Campus Ministry United, 2009, https://campusministryunited.com/Documents/Porn_Again_Christian.pdf.
2. Ann Rule, *The Stranger Beside Me* (Pocket Books, 2009), xiv.
3. Polly Nelson, *Defending the Devil* (William Morrow, 1994), 319, 259.

CHAPTER 13

1. Wikipedia, "Attica Prison Riot," last edited March 1, 2025, https://en.wikipedia.org/wiki/Attica_Prison_riot.

CHAPTER 14

1. Wikipedia, "Kenneth Bianchi," last edited March 1, 2025, https://en.wikipedia.org/wiki/Kenneth_Bianchi.

CHAPTER 15

1. Fox Butterfield, "A Boy Who Killed Coldly Is Now a Prison 'Monster,'" *New York Times*, March 22, 1989, https://www.nytimes.com/1989/03/22/nyregion/a-boy-who-killed-coldly-is-now-a-prison-monster.html.
2. Fox Butterfield, "Jailed 'Monster' Gets More Prison Time for Stabbing a Guard," *New York Times*, April 20, 1989, https://www.nytimes.com/1989/04/20/nyregion/jailed-monster-gets-more-prison-time-for-stabbing-a-guard.html.
3. Fox Butterfield, "Caged for Life, and His Jailers Stand Back," *New York Times*, April 14, 1989, https://www.nytimes.com/1989/04/14/nyregion/caged-for-life-and-his-jailers-stand-back.html.
4. Butterfield, "A Boy Who Killed Coldly Is Now a Prison 'Monster.'"
5. Butterfield, "Jailed 'Monster' Gets More Prison Time for Stabbing a Guard."
6. William Glaberson, "Bosket Loses Federal Court Ruling Over Being Shackled to Cell Door," *New York Times*, June 6, 1989,

Notes

https://www.nytimes.com/1989/06/06/nyregion/bosket-loses-federal-court-ruling-over-being-shackled-to-cell-door.html.
7. Wikipedia, "Willie Bosket," last edited September 13, 2024, https://en.wikipedia.org/wiki/Willie_Bosket.
8. John Eligon, "Two Decades in Solitary," *New York Times*, September 22, 2008, https://www.nytimes.com/2008/09/23/nyregion/23inmate.html.
9. *Criminal*, "Episode 86: Willie Bosket," March 9, 2018, https://thisiscriminal.com/wp-content/uploads/2018/03/Episode-86-Willie-Bosket.pdf.
10. *Criminal*, "Episode 86."
11. "Incarcerated Lookup: Bosket, Willie," New York Department of Corrections and Community Supervision, DIN# 84A6391, accessed March 10, 2025, https://nysdoccslookup.doccs.ny.gov/.

CHAPTER 16

1. Wikipedia, "Charles Manson," last edited March 15, 2025, https://en.wikipedia.org/wiki/Charles_Manson.
2. "The Way Up—Manson Killers Are Born Again," CieloDrive.com, accessed March 20, 2025, https://www.cielodrive.com/archive/the-way-up-manson-killers-are-born-again/.

CHAPTER 18

1. *"Jimmy Lee Gray v. State of Mississippi,"* Supreme Court of Mississippi, September 26, 1979, https://law.justia.com/cases/mississippi/supreme-court/1979/51227-0.html.
2. *"Jimmy Lee Gray v. State of Mississippi."*
3. Michael L. Radelet, "Botched Executions," Death Penalty Information Center, updated February 28, 2024, https://deathpenaltyinfo.org/executions/botched-executions.
4. Associated Press, "Father Says Execution Won't Erase His Memories," *New York Times*, September 3, 1983, https://www.nytimes.com/1983/09/03/us/father-says-execution-won-t-erase-his-memories.html.

CHAPTER 19

1. "Were You There?" song lyrics, public domain.

ABOUT THE AUTHOR

A TEXAS NATIVE, DON Dickerman played college basketball at the University of Texas at Arlington and semipro baseball until a call to ministry led him to seminary. He graduated valedictorian from Trinity Valley Seminary and received a doctor of theology from Phoenix University of Theology.

Having served as a pastor and associate pastor, in 1974 he birthed one of the largest prison ministries in the world, preaching in more than 850 different prisons around the world. He also ministered at two executions. In 1987, Dickerman received a very special anointing for deliverance and healing.

Don and his late wife, Peggy, have two sons, Don Jr. and Rob, who are the pride of his life.

To reach Don Dickerman's ministry, contact:
Liberated Living
3224 Cheek-Sparger Road
Bedford, TX 76021
(817) 581-8860
liberatedliving.info
don@dondickerman.com